Leadership Competency for the Nonprofit Leader

Christopher W. Vetter, Ph.D.

Leadership Competency for the Nonprofit Leader

You can write to the author at cvetter@corban.edu.

A dissertation submitted to the Faculty of the School of Professional Studies of Gonzaga University in partial fulfillment of the requirements for the degree of Doctor of Philosophy.

Additional copies of this volume are available for sale online at
www.CreateSpace.com
www.BooksaMillion.com
www.BarnesandNoble.com
www.Amazon.com

To my family, who for many months waited for this
to be done. This has truly been a family effort.
Thank you for your support and patience.

To all the leaders who serve because they believe in something
bigger than themselves and truly want to make this world a
better place. We do not realize how many of you are
out there and the significance of what you do,
but if you stop leading we would soon know.
Thank you and keep up the good work.

Acknowledgments

Many individuals and groups made contributions to this volume. Their input varied but all were important in their own ways. The faculty and staff at Gonzaga University were a tremendous encouragement through the entire journey.

Special thanks to Dr. Lisa Mazzei for taking on the responsibility of Committee Chair when Dr. Sandra Wilson retired. It is not easy to step into a project already underway. You did a masterful job of shaping the original ideas.

To all the faculty in the Leadership Program—your thoughtful input and care for the development of the students is greatly appreciated. I think more carefully, critically, and hopefully more compassionately about leading because of my time with you.

I also need to acknowledge my fellow students. A few of us developed special friendships along the way. These friendships were an important part of the journey for me. The challenge and encouragement were needed at a variety of points along the way. Thank you.

Finally, there are many people with whom I have worked over the years in a variety of capacities and many different places. You have experienced my blunders and successes as a leader. You have helped me shape not only my leadership values, but also my leadership practices. Thank you for allowing me to learn from your advice, your experience, but also from my successes and mistakes. I am the person I am today because of your input into my life. My hope is that I can do the same for those in my spheres of influence.

Abstract

During the spring of 2011 a group of individuals engaged in a research project intended to learn more about the competencies required for leading social service organizations in the nonprofit sector. The Delphi method was used to gather the input from the panel of 10 individuals beginning with the question "In your opinion, what are the skills, knowledge, traits, motives, and self-concept/self-understanding that are essential for executive-level leaders in nonprofit, social services organizations?" The results were compiled and refined over a total three rounds in which the panel members were able to refine and adjust their responses based on the aggregated results from the Delphi Panel. The result was a list of competencies deemed to be important for those leading social service agencies in the nonprofit sector. While the final competency list had similarities to other models, a key difference was that leaders in nonprofit agencies must have a high level of commitment to the purpose and mission of the organization which they lead.

Keywords: Competency, competency model, Delphi method, nonprofit leadership, leadership competency

Contents

List of Tables

List of Figures

Chapter One

Introduction

The 20th century was a period of significant change in the size and number of North American institutions of all kinds. This period was marked by an expansion of government services, public education at all levels, and the business sector.

Several notable writers have noted that three separate but significant sectors are evident in our society, each making its own contribution. These include the public sector (government), the private sector (business), and most recently, the nonprofit sector (Boris & Steuerle, 2006, p. 67; Drucker, 1994, p. 75; Nanus & Dobbs, 1999, p. 30).

The rapid growth of the nonprofit sector has been a late 20th century phenomenon. Drucker (1996) placed the number of organizations in the nonprofit sector at just under one million. He predicted that the nonprofit sector would become increasingly important in society (p. xiv). Ten years later, Korngold (2006) placed the number of organizations in the nonprofit sector at 1.3 million in the United States (para. 2). The exact number of nonprofits is difficult to determine. Frumkin (2002) placed the number at 1.5 million (p. 8).

The staggering growth of this sector necessitates leadership, especially executive leadership that is capable of guiding a nonprofit organization on a path of sustainability and effectiveness.

The nonprofit sector is generally viewed as being comprised of organizations that have three common organizational features. First, they do not coerce participation in the organization; second, they operate without distributing profits; third, they exist without simple and clear lines of ownership (Frumkin, 2002, p. 3).

Drucker (1994) described nonprofits or the "social sector" as society's means of addressing the social challenges and creating citizenship (pp. 75-76). Though nonprofits serve a variety of purposes, within the North American context, the common denominator is that "funding in excess of expenses" is not expected (Plas & Lewis, 2001, p. xiii). Hence these organizations are not expected to make a financial profit from their operation. They also have tax-exempt status (Werther, 2004, p. 1097).

Nonprofit organizations include social service agencies, trade or professional organizations, civil rights groups, faith-based groups, health care organizations, environmental groups, recreation groups, and political organizations (Boris & Steuerle, 2006, p. 66; Plas & Lewis, 2001, p. xiii; Project Team, 2005). Hammack and Young (1993) noted that nonprofits provide most of the performing arts in the form of classical music, ballet, and modern dance; half or more of hospital care; one-fifth of the places in post-secondary education; two-thirds of the daycare spaces; and most of the vocational training and family counseling delivered in

America (p. 5). The services delivered by nonprofits touch nearly every aspect of life for individuals in the United States, for some on a daily basis.

The challenge facing the nonprofit sector at this point is twofold. First, while increasing demands are being placed on executives in nonprofit organizations, a commensurate level of leadership training material or organizational research that focuses on the nonprofit sector is absent (Bielefeld, 2006, p. 396; Billis, 1993, p. 319). The second challenge nonprofits encounter is that they, along with many other organizations, face significant challenges in finding key leaders due to changing demographics (Barrett & Beeson, 2002, p. 18; Teegarden, 2004, p. 2). The shrinking numbers of those in the age bracket currently providing leadership in all types of organizations will mean stiffer competition for those with the necessary leadership skills and experience. This, coupled with rising expectations for leaders, will result in nonprofits needing to be proactive and intentional as they seek to meet their leadership needs. In addition, nonprofit organizations need to demonstrate their missional effectiveness in order to attract competent leaders (Gelatt, 1992, p. 1; Kaye, 2005, pp. 30-31).

While the leadership challenge for nonprofits is not confined to the executive level, this research will focus on the executive leadership level within the nonprofit sector. Billis (1993) noted that nonprofits face problems related to governance, accountability, organizational change, and understanding how to relate to stakeholders (p. 325-327). If the topic of nonprofit leadership were considered more broadly, all aspects of leadership that are being researched and discussed in the literature could, in most cases, be applicable to the nonprofit sector as well. At the same time, there is a growing level of consideration of what the other sectors could potentially learn from the nonprofit sector (Billis, 1993, p. 320; Bowman, 2003; Drucker, 1989, p. 88; Gelatt, 1992, p. ix; Salamon, 2003, p. 5; Strauss, Rosenheck, D'Aurelio, & Roseheim, 2008, p. 35). Though the challenges and problems related to leadership in each sector have some similarities, the unique nature of the nonprofit sector suggests that the application of management tools, such as a leadership competency model, if described and contextualized, might benefit nonprofit organizations.

This study uses a competency model as an approach to leadership for the nonprofit sector. While the current competency models have much to offer in terms of understanding the competent leader, the unique challenges of nonprofits require careful consideration before adopting a model developed for leadership in a setting other than that of a nonprofit organization. The study results will contribute to a better understanding of the competencies required of leaders who will excel within the nonprofit sector.

Background to the Problem

This next section provides an overview of the nonprofit sector highlighting the rapid development in the 20th century resulting in the current leadership challenges facing the sector. This overview will provide foundation for the purpose of the study and the chosen research methodology.

The Rise of the Nonprofit Sector

Peter Drucker (1994) viewed the rise and expansion of the nonprofit sector as a result of the "social transformation" that has occurred in "developed, free-market countries" (p. 53). Drucker posited that North American society had experienced two major transformations in little more than 100 years. The first was a shift from an agrarian society to an industrial society. This was followed by a transformation from an industrial economy to a knowledge-based economy. While these transformations have, for the most part, been beneficial, there have been significant noneconomic changes.

In terms of how society has changed within the free market economies, Drucker (1994) noted that the needs of society that were once met within the confines of a small, local community are no longer being met because of the societal changes that have taken place. The industrialization of the early 20th century brought about urbanization, which forced people from farms to factories located in cites. While there were problems associated with migration, for the most part industrialization afforded people the opportunity for economic advancement (p. 59). One downside of this migration from farm to factory was the loss of a local community that provided for many of the universal societal needs, such as education, welfare support, healthcare, and care for the less fortunate.

The transition to a knowledge-based economy has continued to exasperate the lack of community that a century ago met these types of needs at the local level. A knowledge economy is marked by a high degree of mobility (Drucker, 1996, p. 74). In response to the question of who takes care of the social challenges in the knowledge society, Drucker explained that this role has fallen to the growing social sector or nonprofit organization (p. 75).

A different perspective in the rise of nonprofits is offered by Hammack and Young (1993), who noted that the foundation of the nonprofit sector in the United States is in the constitutional and political decisions made early in the history of the United States (p. 9). These authors cited Americans' dislike for "powerful central government" and their unwillingness "to pay high taxes at any level of government," adding that Americans "defined what was to be regarded as the public good much more narrowly than did Europeans" (p. 9).

This perspective ties the origin of the strong nonprofit sector in the United States to a series of political decisions rather than to economic development in the form of the Industrial Revolution and resulting sociological developments. Both perspectives on the development of nonprofits in America make important contributions to an understanding of nonprofits. All the factors offered have played some role in the development and growth of the nonprofit sector, making it what it is today.

This background helps us to understand why the nonprofit sector has experienced significant growth, and why it will continue to grow and play a significant role not only in life in the United States, but also in other countries (Hammack & Young, 1993, p. 4). While some would envision that the social challenges faced in the 21st century could be met by government or perhaps business, the constitutional and political restraints placed on the American federal government in comparison with its European counterparts makes this unlikely. This situation is most notable in the First Amendment "establishment" clause that forbids the federal government from supporting religion in a way that was seen in Europe. This clause eliminated the primary arrangement used in Europe for many years to support education, social services, health care, the arts, and relief to the poor (p. 10). In place of this arrangement, the nonprofit sector, though it was not called that, flourished in the United States for two reasons. The first was the distrust Americans had for strong central government (Hammack & Young, 1993, p. 10). The second was economic. Having services such as education and care of the poor delivered in the most inexpensive manner was common in colonial America (Hall, 2006, p. 34).

The growth of the nonprofit sector is furthered evidenced by the fact that 70% of the one million nonprofit organizations that existed in the early 1990s had come into existence in the last 30 years. Most had some type of community services focus and sought to address some type of social problem (Drucker, 1994, p. 75). Many of the purposes these organizations were created to address still exist today and, if anything, have become more acute. In all likelihood, the growth of single-issue organizations will continue (Eisenberg, 2004). This type of growth necessitates the development of leadership on a large scale to meet the needs in this expanding sector that strives to meet a broad range of needs within our society.

Leadership Needs of the Nonprofit Sector

There is a trend in nonprofit organizations of striving for professionalization, illustrated by the utilization of management techniques such as strategic planning, financial analysis, public relations, and computerized databases. This striving for professionalization is due in part to the need for greater efficiency in constituencies that are asking for demonstrable success of stated outcomes (Billis, 1993, p. 321; Nanus & Dobbs, 1999, p. 47).

The concern for demonstrable success in nonprofit organizations has contributed to the overlap of management techniques used by profits and nonprofits. Some may question this professionalization, but building an organization that is responsive to the needs of its constituency while being highly innovative will require new ways of doing things (Carbone, 1993, p. 295; Nanus & Dobbs, 1999, p. 50).

This professionalization has led to changing expectations for those who lead within the nonprofit organization. Dedication and commitment to the cause are no longer sufficient grounds for being placed in a leadership position; leaders must have a certain level of professionalism to succeed (Bryne, 1990).

The top leaders in nonprofits must now be able to manage relationships with diverse constituencies, as well as implement and utilize management techniques in organizations unfamiliar with these processes. The breadth of this type of mandate for nonprofit leaders can seem daunting. Successful leadership in this type of environment will require the advancement of individuals with a unique set of abilities.

The growth within the nonprofit sector will create the need for an increasing number of executive-level leaders. Based on the projected growth, another 300,000 nonprofit organizations could exist by 2016, and along with that growth a corresponding need for leadership will arise (Tierney, 2006, p. 14).

This challenge will be heightened by the leadership shortage felt in all types of organizations. A report released by The Conference Board, an organization that does business-related research, noted that one of the key challenges that will be faced by business organization in 2010 is finding individuals who are capable of leading organizations (Barrett & Beeson, 2002, p. 12).

The demands of leading within the anticipated business environment will necessitate viewing leadership less as the task of a single individual and more as something that arises from within the framework of a team that has been established for the purpose of leading (p. 13).

An increase in the number of nonprofit organizations is not the only factor contributing to the leadership challenges within this sector. Strong evidence indicates that a significant number of current executives in nonprofit organizations are poised to transition in the near future.

A survey conducted in 2004 of 9,000 nonprofit organizations in the United States revealed that there will be more transitions at the executive-leadership level in the next five than there have been in the previous 10 years (Teegarden, 2004, p. 4). Sixty-five percent of the executives surveyed indicated that they planned to leave their current posts by 2009 (p. 4). A survey conducted by DRG in 2006 had similar results, reporting that 40%

of responding CEOs planned to leave their positions by 2008 (Development Resource Group Inc., 2008). Couple this dynamic with a lack of attention given to succession planning, and the leadership challenges for nonprofits can be considered significant as this large scale leadership transition takes place (Development Resource Group Inc., 2008; Seel, 2006, p. iii).

It is expected that this large-scale transition will effect smaller nonprofits in a greater way than it will larger nonprofit organizations (Teegarden, 2004, p. 8). One conclusion of the report's author was that "the sector is moving from relative stability to instability at the top" (p. 9). For those who work within the nonprofit sector, the coming years, according to Teegarden, will require a greater level of attention to filling executive level leadership roles than before. This shift will need to take place when demographics indicate that fewer candidates will be available for the positions needing to be filled. Possessing a clear understanding of the competencies required to lead in a nonprofit setting will aid in the development and recruitment of the leaders needed by nonprofits in the coming years.

There is much discussion in current leadership literature, especially recent journal articles, on the topic of leadership competencies and competency models (for example (Davis, Naughton, & Rothwell, 2004; Mansfield, 2004; Rothwell & Wellins, 2004; Le Deist & Winterton, 2005; Ruth, 2006; Brownell & Goldsmith, 2006; Yu-fen & Tsui-chih, 2007; Bryson, Ackermann, & Eden, 2007).

One challenge faced by the reader is to understand the intended context and the meaning ascribed to the concept of *competence.* Grasping the concept of competency requires an understanding of how this vast array of definitions and models fit together to form a broader picture of leadership and, in this case, the role of the executive leader in a nonprofit organization. The definitions of competency can cover not only the skills and knowledge but the attitudes, values and motivations of leaders as well.

The first mention of competence used to describe characteristics associated with superior performance was attributed to Robert W. White in a 1959 journal article (Le Deist & Winterton, 2005, p. 31). In this article entitled "Motivation Reconsidered: The Concept of Competence," White proposed a connection between cognitive competence and motivational action tendencies. White defined competence as an "organism's capacity to interact effectively with its environment" (White, 1959, p. 297). White viewed people as being highly capable of developing greater levels of competence and wanted to understand the motivational aspects of competence development. White's work opened the door for the study of competence as an aspect of human development related to performance in the workplace.

The North American fascination with measurement and prediction found expression in the wave of testing that emerged in the post-war era of the 1950s. Intelligence and aptitude testing were widely used in the United States by the 1960s and 1970s. Standardized testing was used in most schools, and entrance exams such as the Scholastic Aptitude Test (SAT) were the norm for all students wishing to pursue higher education. McClelland noted that if size, influence and profitability were the measure of success, then the American testing movement could be deemed a success (McClelland, 1973, p. 1). During this period, it was common for intelligence or aptitude tests to be used as a means of predicting future vocational success. McClelland challenged this use of intelligence testing on the basis of the tests' validity, which he described as being "by no means so overwhelming as most of us, rather unthinkingly, had come to think it was" (p. 1). McClelland's contention was that aptitude testing was a great predictor of future grades or performance in an educational setting, but their use for anything more, such as predicting success in professional roles, was not warranted. McClelland further noted that research conducted on the academic achievement in college of individuals engaged in scientific research did not find that higher grades in college meant success as a researcher (p. 2). McClelland argued that aptitude or intelligence tests were an inadequate means of measuring job success.

The alternative suggested by McClelland (1973) was that a new way of testing be developed that would test for competence, not intelligence (p. 7). This proposed change in testing focus became the source for much of the current research-based competency modeling that is in use today and has resulted in the development of over 300 behavioral event interview-based competency models. As of 1991, the competency assessment method was used by more than 100 researchers in 24 countries (Spencer, McClelland, & Spencer, 1994, p. 19). Competency now looks not only at performance but at the motives, values, and other personal characteristics that influence individual performance in the workplace. There is a growing recognition that motives, traits, and other personal characteristics need to be part of the competency models as well (Boyatzis, 1983, p. 34).

The Need for Further Research

The size and unique role of the nonprofit sector has begun to attract the attention of those concerned with leadership and leadership development. ==The need for qualified and effective leaders will only continue to grow as the nonprofit sector itself continues to grow.== This growing awareness of the need for competent leaders within the nonprofit sector has been noted by Eisenberg (2004, para. 1) as well as by Hailey and James (2004, p. 344). Much of the current research and writing in the field of leadership is geared to business or government (Billis, 1993, p. 319; Block, 2001, p. 97; Hailey & James, 2004, p. 345; Nanus & Dobbs, 1999, p. 11). This orientation does not mean that the research and writing are of no value to leaders in nonprofit setting. Many of the ideas, principles, and models are useful in a nonprofit setting as well. What is lacking is research that focuses on the unique challenges and needs of an individual leading a nonprofit. Zarinpoush and Hall (2007) noted that little is known about the perspective that nonprofit leaders have of their organizations, the challenges faced by nonprofits, and the important role they have within society (p. 4).

If the growing nonprofit sector in North America is to continue to thrive, it will require leaders with the competencies to match the unique purposes and context of the nonprofit organization. What is absent in the literature is a well-defined,

aptitude
vs competency

25

validated set of competencies for a leader within the nonprofit sector.

This study will investigate the background and current use of competency models with the goal of establishing a competency model for executive leaders within the social service context of the nonprofit sector. The lack of competency models for leaders within the nonprofit sector means that leadership recruitment and development within these sectors must rely either on competencies models developed for other contexts, or on other means of evaluating leadership readiness and development.

The context in which one manages is a significant factor that cannot be overlooked when considering a leader's competence (Robertson & Gibbons, 1999, p. 5; Spencer & Spencer, 1993, p. 201). While various studies have presented competency models aimed at human services (education and health care), the breadth of the nonprofit sector is not represented in these models (p. 201). Generic competency models for managers are helpful in establishing broad parameters, but these models are lacking when sector-specific issues and a particular level within an organization are taken into consideration. It has been documented that competencies vary depending on the level at which an individual may be working in a given organization (Spencer & Spencer, 1993, p. 214), and on whether performance or "promotability" (Robertson & Gibbons, 1999, p. 12) is being considered. Having a sector-specific competency model focused on a particular level will aid the recruitment and development of individuals to meet the growing leadership needs within the nonprofit sector.

The role of the executive leader within a nonprofit setting requires additional research from which to build a better understanding of the demands and expectations placed on nonprofit leaders. It has been noted that the context in which a leader functions has significant influence on how leadership is carried out. It therefore cannot be assumed that the research pertaining to leadership in for-profit settings will be applicable to those leading nonprofits. Understanding the differences between the profit, public, and nonprofit leadership is critical in ensuring the success not only of the leaders themselves, but also of the organizations that they lead.

What has been become evident in recent years is that the nonprofit sector is facing a massive turnover in leadership at the highest levels. This observation applies to both the United States and Canada (Zarinpoush & Hall, 2007, p. 10). What does not seem to have been addressed at this writing in 2010 is a strategy by which these vacancies can be filled in a timely fashion with individuals who possess the competencies required to lead effectively within the nonprofit sector. The research to date is lacking in the area of identifying the competencies required of a nonprofit leader. Moreover, not enough research has been done that focuses on the nonprofit executive in the emerging context to determine whether the existing competency models for leaders and managers are adequate for the next generation of nonprofit leaders. Further research regarding the applicability of current competency models to nonprofits would help meet the challenge of identifying or developing the leadership needed in the nonprofit sector in the coming years. If there is confidence in a competency model related to nonprofit executives, those responsible for the selection and development of leadership can move forward in a more deliberate fashion. This position will enable nonprofit organizations to shorten the amount of time required in a leadership transition, thereby contributing to greater organizational effectiveness.

In addition to research aimed at understanding the competencies required for a nonprofit leader, research aimed at creating a greater level of understanding of the nonprofit sector among the general public has been identified by Canadian nonprofit executives as an area of priority (Zarinpoush & Hall, 2007, p. 16). These researchers indicated that the public does not have a good understanding of the work done by nonprofits. Some executives also suggested that many within the nonprofit sector itself have not "internalized the value of their work" (pp. 16-17). This theory would point to a need for even those with a high level of participation in a nonprofit setting to better understand the significance of the contribution made to society by nonprofit organizations. The contributions to quality of life and meeting of social needs within North American society are poorly understood at best.

Although it would be very difficult to quantify the contributions made by nonprofits in communities and settings all across the country, apart from a dollar amount spent, there is also little research that points to results or outcomes of the efforts made by nonprofits. Within the business realm, the success of a company can be measured by profitability. The measure of success for a nonprofit can be more elusive and context-dependent, which means a variety of methods are needed to measure outcomes. In an attempt to provide some type of objective measure, nonprofits are adapting and adopting various metrics used in the business community (Frumkin, 2002, p. 23). Salamon (2003) observed that the while management techniques used in business are being used by nonprofits, some of the primary principles of operation for nonprofits, such as maintaining a clear mission, serving clients well, and having a staff committed to organizational purpose, have been making their way into the for-profit sector (p. 5). Further research in this area could be very valuable to the nonprofit sector as they compete with the public and private sectors for the people with leadership skills who will be needed in increasing numbers in those contexts as well. If a strong case can be built for the notion that nonprofits contribute significantly to the life of a given community or area, people will be more likely to engage with the nonprofit sector in a variety of ways that could include everything from financial contribution, to volunteerism, to involvement at the senior leadership level, which is becoming more of a challenge.

Study Purpose

The purpose of this study is to establish a competency model for executive leaders within the social service segment of the nonprofit sector. The social service sector has been defined as "social care provided to deprived, neglected, or handicapped children and youth, the needy, elderly, the mentally ill and developmentally disabled, and disadvantaged adults. These services include daycare, counseling, job training, child protection, foster care, residential treatment, homemakers, rehabilitation, and sheltered workshops" (Smith, 2002, p. 153). Salamon (2001) estimated that social service agencies comprise close to 40% of all nonprofit service agencies (p. 31). Input and feedback from those currently or recently in leadership positions is used to identify, from a practitioner's perspective, the competencies required for effective leadership within the nonprofit sector. Using this information, a competency model can be developed to foster the recognition and development of the identified competencies for nonprofit leaders.

The research questions that flow from the purpose of this study are:

Research question #1: What competencies are needed for executives to lead effectively in the social service organization in the nonprofit sector?

Research question #2: How do the competencies as identified by leaders in a particular nonprofit sector compare with competencies lists formulated for similar roles in other sectors?

Research question #3: Can a set of competencies unique to nonprofit organizations be identified for use in recruitment and development of nonprofit leaders?

Overview of Research Methods

The study will incorporate the Delphi method, which was first used by the RAND Corporation in the 1950s as a means of forecasting or predicting through the use of experts in a particular field (Linstone & Turoff, 2002a, p. 10). This method was developed for use in areas in which there was not any established data or common foundational knowledge that allowed for predictive modeling. Dalkey and Helmer (1963) published one of the first papers that outlined the technique as it had been used at the RAND corporation in the development of defense strategy during the Cold War period. The object of this methodology was "to obtain the most reliable consensus of opinion of a group of experts" (p. 458). The Delphi method or exercise, as it was originally used, sought to educe an expert's reasoning behind his or her response to the primary question, understand the factors that were considered by the expert in that response, and understand how the factors were considered in the formulation of the response. Finally, Delphi was used in an attempt to learn about new or different information that may be salient to the discussion (p. 458).

Since these studies in the early 1950s, the Delphi method has moved beyond the defense sector to every major sector and geographic location (Linstone & Turoff, 2002a, p. 11; Wells, 1988, p. 68). A review of literature demonstrates that the Delphi method has been used extensively in health care (Hasson, Keeney, & McKenna, 2000; Holmes, 2005) and education (Hayes, 2007; Wells, 1988). It has also been used in other fields such as marketing (Larreche & Montgomery, 1977) and the development of leadership competency models (Gliddon, 2006). Linstone and Turoff (2002) noted that the geographic spread of Delphi is virtually worldwide and that the method has been used in most sectors, including academe (p. 11). The Delphi method appears to have experienced widespread adoption as a research technique and as a method of knowledge integration for the benefit of a larger body (Okhuysen & Eisenhardt, 2002, p. 371).

While the Delphi method is not without its critics, it does allow for the input of a geographically dispersed group of experts to be pooled and refined to a point of greater consensus around a given topic. While there can be great variety in the methodological details in the use of Delphi, the basic structure as outlined can be applied successfully to a wide range of questions and contexts. The research questions asked in this study are well suited to the Delphi methodology due to a lack of foundational research in the area of leadership competency models for nonprofit leaders within the social sector, and to the methodology's allowing for the gathering of input from a geographically (and potentially philosophically) diverse group of experts.

Operational Definition of Terms

Private, public, nonprofit sectors

Modern economies are comprised of three primary sectors. These are the business or the for-profit sector; the government sector; and the nonprofit sector (Werther, 2004, p. 1097).

Nonprofit organizations

These consist of a variety of organizations that have three common organizational features. First, they do not coerce participation; second, they operate without distributing profits; and third, they exist without simple and clear lines of ownership (Frumkin, 2002, p. 3). Drucker (1994) describes nonprofits or the "social sector" as society's means of addressing the social challenges and creating citizenship (pp. 75-76). Though nonprofits serve a variety of purposes, within the North American context the common denominator is that "funding in excess of expenses" is not expected (Plas & Lewis, 2001, p. xiii). Hence, nonprofits are not expected to make a financial profit from their operation. They also have tax-exempt status (Werther, 2004, p. 1097).

Social services agency within the nonprofit sector

A social services agency is a subsection of the nonprofit sector. The term "social services agency" is being used in reference to that portion of the nonprofit sector that provides services to the "deprived, neglected, or handicapped children and youth, the needy, elderly, the mentally ill and developmentally disabled, and disadvantaged adults. These services include daycare, counseling, job training, child protection, foster care, residential treatment, homemakers, rehabilitation, and sheltered workshops" (Smith, 2002, p. 153).

Competent

An individual is deemed competent when he or she is able to accomplish a given task effectively (Woodruffe, 1991 as cited in Le Deist & Winterton, 2005).

Competencies

These are specific statements that define areas of expertise viewed as essential for success in a given context. These would include competency characteristics or capabilities such as motives, traits, self-concept, knowledge, and skills (Spencer & Spencer, 1993, pp. 9-11). The motives and self concept in competency include a self-awareness that includes a realistic view of personal strengths and weaknesses along with personal goals and values (Lowney, 2003, p. 98).

Competency models

Competency models are the collection of competency statements for a given role that take into consideration not only behavioral aspects of leading, but also the necessary knowledge, skills, personal traits, and motives along with the organization's strategy and its implications for the leadership needs of the organization (Barner, 2000, p. 48; Boyatzis, 1983, p. 21, p. 35; Le Deist & Winterton, 2005, p. 33).

Overview of the Dissertation

The second chapter of this dissertation contains an overview of the literature related to the two broad topics of this study. There is a review of literature regarding the background and current state of the nonprofits in general, and the development of the competency movement as it influences the current study. Chapter III describes the research methodology employed in this study. This description includes a brief background on Delphi, in addition to the data collection and analysis methods used in this study. Chapter IV contains the results of the data analysis, and Chapter V provides the conclusions, recommendations, and responses gleaned from the data in relation to the three research questions of this study.

Chapter Two

Literature Review

The literature review builds the theoretical foundation of leadership competency as it is found in various disciplines and fields, with particular attention to the nonprofit sector in North America. An understanding of the background and current practices regarding the use of leadership competency models is necessary as a competency model for nonprofit leaders is explored.

The first section of this chapter explores not only the background of the nonprofit sector in North America, but also the various ways in which the roles, responsibilities, and expectations of executive leadership in nonprofit organizations are viewed within current leadership literature. The difference between leading in a profit setting versus a nonprofit setting will be explored as well. The contributions of servant leadership to nonprofit leadership roles are reviewed in this section.

The second section of this review describes the background and development of competency, and the various ways in which it is currently discussed in the leadership literature seeking to develop a holistic understanding of competency. Competency models and how they are utilized in various settings will be presented as well. The third section presents information on the limited use competency frameworks have had within the nonprofit sector.

The History and Development of Nonprofits in the United States

Nonprofit organizations have been a part of the societal landscape in the United States in some form since the country's inception. They have served to educate, heal, aid in time of disaster, provide for basic needs, and give emotional and spiritual comfort in a variety of ways through the years.

Salamon (2003) noted, "If the nonprofit sector is one of the most important components of American life, it is also one of the least understood" (p. 7).

Having an appropriate understanding of the nonprofit sector in all its complexity is foundational to meeting the challenges ahead.

Definitions and Roles of Nonprofit Organizations

Many names have been used to define this group of organizations that are not privately or publicly owned businesses or part of the government. Terms such as nonprofits, third sector, independent sector, tax exempt, nongovernmental organization (NGO), and more recently "the commons," have all been used to describe the group of organizations at some point (Frumkin, 2002, pp. 10-14). For the purpose of this research, the terms "nonprofit sector" or "nonprofit organizations" were employed because both are widely used and understood.

The common characteristics of nonprofit organizations include the following: Participation of members is voluntary; nonprofits do not distribute profits to stakeholders or operate with the purpose of financial gain; nonprofits exist without clear lines of ownership; and they have a mandate related to some type of identified societal need (Frumkin, 2002, p. 3; Plas & Lewis, 2001, p. xiii; Werther, 2004, p. 1097).

Nonprofits are also defined by their position within society, which has three main sectors: business, government, and nonprofits. Any organization run for financial profit fits within the frame of the first sector. All government-run enterprises fit within the second sector.

The third sector include those organizations that are neither controlled by the government nor run with a primary purposes of making financial profit (Cameron, 2004). In the United States, this group is also referred to as the independent sector and is comprised of organizations that fall into one of two tax-exempt categories: 501(c)(3) charitable and religious organizations, and 501(c)(4) social welfare organizations (Weitzman, Jalandoni, Lampkin, & Pollack, 2002, xxvii).

Contributions of the Nonprofit Sector to Society

The contribution of nonprofits to the whole of society can be seen through the various roles that they fulfill. Nonprofits are service providers, as evidenced by the fact that 50% of the nation's hospitals, 1/3 of the health clinics, and 46% of the higher education institutions are nonprofit (Salamon, 2003, p. 11). Nonprofits have also had a role in advocacy by identifying unaddressed needs and bring them to the attention of society, advocating for solutions. Over the years, causes such as women's suffrage, civil rights, environmental issues, gay rights, and the conservative movement have all begun within the nonprofit sector.

The nonprofit sector fulfills the need felt by many people to express themselves in the areas of art, religion, recreation, and culture. This need may be met by opera companies, book clubs, sport leagues for youth, symphonies, and churches or synagogues. Nonprofits also play a role in community building. They make an important contribution in building what has been referred to as social capital. Social capital is the trust and reciprocity necessary for the smooth functioning of the market economy. Working together in organizations around common interests builds trust that carries over to other functions within society (Salamon, 2002, p. 11).

Nonprofits have also had a role in promoting the values of both individualism, and solidarity with others in society. Through participation in and involvement with the causes undertaken by nonprofit organizations, individuals find expression of personal values. Working together through nonprofits teaches that people can accept and embrace responsibilities beyond themselves, extending to the community in which they live and society as a whole. Participating in nonprofits accomplishes a greater purpose than just the stated organizational purpose; participating also gives opportunity to learn about and exhibit good citizenship. People need to express their faith, values, and commitments. Participation in nonprofit organizations allows people to act on what is most important to them (Frumkin, 2002, p. 96). Without the volunteerism driven by the deep-seated personal values of the participants, nonprofit organizations could not operate or function. Nonprofit organizations, especially in the form of foundations, offer the wealthy an opportunity to "give back" to the society (Fleishman, 2007, p. 35).

When it comes to meeting the needs of society, the nonprofit sector has developed different types of organizations to meet certain needs. The charitable organization has traditionally been responsible for meeting people's physical needs, such as those for food, shelter, and clothing (Steinberg & Powell, 2006, p. 2). Another class of nonprofit organizations that has met the needs of society is mutual benefit organizations. These include unions, trade associations, professional associations, and social clubs. The benefits provided by this group of organizations have been directed more intentionally toward the members of the organizations and less toward those outside the organizations. This does not, however, mean that there are no benefits for nonmembers. Professional associations provide training and credentials important to maintain public safety and trust in a given profession. This service does benefit all of society.

The benefits to society are also economic. The numbers at the national level show a sector with considerable strength. The nonprofit sector employed nearly 11 million paid workers in 1998, representing 7% of the entire American workforce (Salamon, 2002, p. 7). This figure does not include volunteers, who numbered 5.6 million. The salaries paid by the nonprofit sector were 6.7% of the national total of $7.27 trillion in 1998 (Weitzman, Jalandoni, Lampkin, & Pollack, 2002, p. 13). These statistics do not take into consideration the contributions of foundations, which awarded grants totaling $33.6 billion in 2005 (Fleishman, 2007, p. 27). This pattern is expected to continue and is likely to grow.

These benefits provided to society by nonprofits are easy to highlight. There is however also a dark side to nonprofits as in any other organization. The individuals leading nonprofit organizations, though they may be motivated to help and serve the less fortunate, can still engage in behaviors that cause problems for them personally and their organizations. These problematic behaviors can range from illegal activity such as embezzlement to poor management of resources (Tropman & Shaefer, 2004, p. 162). These issues can arise from the personal causes on the part of staff but it has also been asserted that structural causes contribute to the failure of nonprofit leaders and their organizations as well (p.163). Tropman cited eight high profile examples of nonprofit executives who engaged in some type of activity that resulted in their removal and some type of damage to their organization. The activities ranged from abuse of power, to embezzlement, and mismanagement (p. 164-165).

Historical Development of Nonprofit Organizations

Different theories in the literature highlight a variety of perspectives on the development of nonprofit organizations in North America. These theories view the development from a variety of perspectives, such as the sociological, the political, and the economic, showing how changes that have taken place on these and other levels have influenced the development and growth of the nonprofit sector. The nonprofit sector has seen greater development in response to unmet needs that individuals and groups of individuals have sought to address by banding together around a common cause.

The notion of caring for those in need exemplified by the modern nonprofit sector has roots in ancient societies. The Code of Hammurabi and Old Testament both contain injunctions designed to protect the less fortunate of the community, with special emphasis on caring for widows and orphans (Block, 2001, p. 98).

Block noted that "religious doctrine, ideology and influence on giving, compassion, and personal sacrifice are a significant part of the heritage of charity and philanthropy" that formed the foundation for the modern nonprofit (p. 98). This religious influence can be seen in the Judeo-Christian tradition, in which instructions are given for the care of the widows, the orphans, and those generally in need (Robbins, 2006, p. 14).

Ancient Egyptians of means offer another example of charity influenced by religious beliefs. Those with wealth were buried with riches, but also with records of those they had helped during their lifetimes. These actions were viewed as a means of petitioning the gods for a restful afterlife, based on good deeds (Block, 2001, p. 98).

The ideals of philanthropy were visible in Greek society as well. Those with wealth would make gifts of things such as theaters and stadiums. This phenomenon represented a shift from giving that benefited a single individual to giving for the good entire community. This practice foreshadowed the current custom of many modern foundations (Block, 2001, p. 98; Robbins, 2006, p. 15).

An important influence in early American practice of charity was the passage of the English Poor Laws, or the Statute of Charitable Uses, in 1601 (Block, 2001, p. 99). The breakup of the feudal system and the influence of the Reformation, which led to the dismantling of Catholic charities in Protestant countries, changed European society (Robbins, 2006, p. 24). These events weakened the hold of the Church and fragmented the civil government, which in turn led to all types of societal and cultural changes in Europe. The areas of education, care for the poor, and care for the ill were some of the areas of society that underwent significant transformation. In an effort to clarify responsibility for the care of the poor, the English Parliament passed the Poor Laws which outlined the responsibilities of relatives, local government, and the broader public responsibility (Block, 2001, p.99).

The early American colonial approach to charity and care for the poor was heavily influenced by the English Poor Laws. This stance, coupled with the aversion of the colonists to government interference, led to work with the poor being done at the local level, often through religious organizations. This desire to be free of government influence has led to the U.S.'s having a larger nonprofit sector than most other industrialized nations (Fleishman, 2007, p. 18).

Gelatt (1992) spoke of the observation by Alexis de Tocqueville that volunteerism was widespread and that there was an unwillingness on the part of Americans to have everything controlled by business or government (p. 2). This attitude has contributed to the strength and size of the nonprofit sector. It is through the nonprofit sector that Americans are able to express and live out their views and values on a wide range of things such as religion, art, education, and social issues without the interference of government (Hammack & Young, 1993, p. 1)

The importance of the nonprofit sector to American society has been evidenced by the privileged position of the sector in relation to taxes levied, or in this case not levied, on nonprofits by government at all levels. It was in 1894 that the federal government first wrote into the law the tax exemption for nonprofit organizations (Block, 2001, p. 104).

The federal government has continued to give nonprofit organizations of all types tax-exempt status, and in 1954 it passed the legislation creating the 501(c)(3) and 501(c)(4) status for organizations. Not only have these organizations been exempt from taxes, but donors to tax-exempt organizations also receive a personal tax deduction. Though there is tax incentive for donating to nonprofit organizations, giving to American charities comprises less than 2% of personal income (Salamon, 2002, p. 51).

It has been noted that explosive growth in the number of nonprofit organizations, from 13,000 in 1940 to over 1.5 million at the end of the century, corresponds with the favorable tax status given to the organizations and those who support them (Hall, 2006, p. 32). The growth and health of the nonprofit sector can be viewed as being influenced, at the very least, by government legislation.

Theories of Development

A number of theories have been put forth to explain the development of the nonprofit sector in the United States and beyond. The theories summarized here included the sociological development theory, the institutional failure theory (which encompasses the three-failure theory), and the constitutional theory.

Sociological Theory

An example of a sociological theory demonstrating the rise of the nonprofit sector was proposed by Peter Drucker. He viewed the expansion of the nonprofit sector in recent history as a necessary third sector in the emerging and developing knowledge society (Drucker, 1994, p. 75). Society has shifted from being primarily agricultural, with people living in small communities where social needs such as education, care for the poor, medical care, and other needs of the individual were dealt with at the local community level, to being an industrial and, more recently, a knowledge society (p. 73). Whereas friends and family once lived in close proximity to one another and worked together to meet needs as they arose, societal shifts have meant that the small communities where these needs were met at a local and personal level are no longer as prevalent. The result has been the development of new mechanisms to meet the social needs of a highly mobile knowledge society. Drucker viewed this change in society as a significant factor in the expansion and growth of the nonprofit sector. The nonprofit sector, while it has been in existence since the coming of the colonists, has become a more crucial element in meeting societal needs, and in providing opportunity for citizenship and belonging in a mobile population (p. 76). The meeting of human needs is certainly a worthy undertaking to be applauded. However, the proliferation of nonprofits has resulted in a patchwork of organizations which can duplicate services which, in the end, is a poor uses of already scarce resources.

Institutional Failure Theory

The three-failure theory or institutional failure theory has been used to explain how failure by any of the three sectors to provide the goods and services needed by society will result in one of the other sectors meeting the need. In this theory, failure by each sector has been evaluated separately. The government failure theory asserts that nonprofit organizations are present in society due to some type of failure on the part of the government to meet the needs of the population in a manner that is deemed appropriate (Steinberg, 2006, p. 122; Young, 2001b, p. 190). There may be a variety of factors that keep the government from meeting the needs of a given group, but the failure to meet the need results in action taken. An example would be the lack of adequate police service. An individual may install a personal security system in an effort to address the need. The formation of a neighborhood watch program as a nonprofit entity illustrates the next level of response and government failure theory in action. The formation of a nonprofit body to provide any service already offered by the government, such as education for children, soup kitchens, or homeless shelters, is an illustration of this theory in practice.

The next element of the three-failure theory is the contract failure theory. This has also been called market failure (Steinberg, 2006, p. 119). Contract failure theory explained the existence of the nonprofits as a natural outcome of the inability of the consumer to judge the quality or quantity of the services received. This has resulted in opportunity for nonprofits organizations (Hammack & Young, 1993, p. 7). The source of this contract or market failure is a condition called *information asymmetry,* in which those who provide a product have more information about the product than the consumer (Young, 2001a, p. 193). A certain amount of information asymmetry ought to be expected. If, however, consumers feel they know too little about a product or cannot obtain the information needed, they will be more reluctant to make a purchase. Several different solutions exist for this condition, one of which is provision of the service or product by a nonprofit organization.

Since nonprofit organizations do not exist solely to make money, the assumption is made that they are less likely to pressure those requiring their services to purchase from them rather than from a competitor (Young, 2001a, p. 194). Young also mentioned that nonprofits are viewed as more trustworthy because of the selection and screening process used when hiring those in leadership roles. Those hired for leadership roles in nonprofits are viewed as being more altruistic than their counterparts in business and therefore more trustworthy, leading to full disclosure related to their products and services. Young noted the governance structure of nonprofits, in which a higher degree of involvement of donors and consumers leads to a higher level of transparency. The summation is that nonprofit organizations are viewed as more trustworthy and therefore less susceptible to contract failure due to information asymmetry.

The third element of the three-failure theory has been referred to as voluntary sector failure (Steinberg, 2006, p. 125). This theory stated that failures, for a variety of reasons, of nonprofit organizations result in either the government or the market taking responsibility for the unmet needs. Reasons for the failures of nonprofits can include having too narrow of a focus, not accurately assessing the needs of clients, and being "amateuristic" or lacking fully credentialed workers (p. 125). This element of the three-failure theory does not explain why the nonprofit sector has grown, but it illustrates the interconnectedness of the three sectors.

Constitutional Theory

Finally, the constitutional theory acknowledged that other forces have been instrumental in the formation and development of the nonprofit sector in the United States. The constitutional theory asserted that the development of nonprofits in the United States has been aided by unique and specific constitutional provisions, such as the separation of powers, the inability of the government to establish any one church, and the limitation on the size of government (Hammack & Young, 1993, pp. 9-10). A deliberate decision to separate church and state put the United States on a different political and social trajectory from that of its European counterparts. The political and economic favor given to nonprofit organizations has led to a much stronger nonprofit sector than in other industrialized countries (p. 10). These are some of the theories that contribute to a broader understanding of the development and status of the nonprofit sector in the United States in 2010.

Challenges Facing the Nonprofit Sector

A review of the literature regarding the challenges faced by the nonprofit sector has revealed a few notable themes. These are diverse in nature, but many of them relate to the leadership and leadership practices in nonprofit organizations. The challenges evaluated in this project have focused on leadership issues for those involved in the nonprofit sector.

One of the greatest challenges faced by nonprofits is finding qualified candidates for leadership roles. A 2009 survey of current leaders of nonprofit organizations with revenues of more than one million dollars found that 57% anticipated more or much more difficulty in filling leadership vacancies (Simms, 2009, p. 16). Similar results were noted in a Watson Wyatt report that found that more than 50% of companies are concerned with keeping or hiring employees with critical skills needed in their company in the next three to five years (Watson Wyatt Worldwide, 2009b, p. 8). The projected need within the nonprofit sector in the 12 months following January 2009 was for 24,000 senior level managers (Simms, 2009, p. 4). The 2008 downturn in the economy has slowed the retirement of the baby boomers, but many are still retiring. A number of recent studies have noted that many people are now planning on a later retirement date than planned, mostly for economic reasons (Brown, 2009, p. 8;

Helman, Copeland, & VanDerhei, 2009, p. 14; Watson Wyatt Worldwide, 2009a, p. 4; Watson Wyatt Worldwide, 2009b, p. 8). This observation stands in contrast to the need for senior level leaders being projected. One possible explanation for this seeming contradiction in the nonprofit sector may be the combination of baby boomer retirements and the need for more leadership due to growth in the nonprofit sector. Simms' (2009) study found that 22% of the senior managers hired by nonprofit organizations in 2008 were hired for newly created positions (p.4).

The need for more leaders at senior levels has been noted in the field of education as well. Rowley (2007) highlighted the need for the development of a competency model for community college presidents as a means of identifying and training future presidents. It is expected that by 2011, 79% of those serving in 2001 will have retired or stepped down (p. 1).

Another challenge identified by this study was the inability of nonprofits to fill leadership vacancies from within the organization. This was evidenced by the reported results, which stated that only 25% of the leadership vacancies filled between June 2007 and December 2008 were taken up by internal candidates (Simms, 2009, p. 4). This stands in sharp contrast with results of visionary companies who, over their collective history, hired only 3.54% of their CEOs from outside the company (Porras & Collins, 1994, p. 173). Simms (2009) noted in a report published by Bridgespan that cultural fit was critical to the success of any leader in a nonprofit organization (p. 9). Hiring people from within the organization can minimize if not eliminate the issue of cultural fit. The matter of cultural fit was identified as one of the four main challenges faced by nonprofits organizations when seeking to fill their current future senior leadership needs.

The four factors cited in the Bridgespan report (Simms, 2009) that make hiring in nonprofits challenging are as follows: 1) There is a lack of candidates with experience and knowledge necessary in leading large nonprofit organizations; 2) Nonprofits face significant salary limitations; 3) There is competition for talent from other organizations in the sector; and 4) It is difficult to find people who fit the culture and mission of the organization(Simms, 2009, p. 10). It was suggested that one way of meeting the challenge of cultural fit was for the organization to expand their ideas of what cultural fit may entail. This will require hiring committees to evaluate the skills, abilities, and experience a candidate brings and to assess whether the candidate has the ability to learn the culture rather than coming as an exact fit (p. 17). This is an area in which a competency model could prove helpful in assessing overall fit between a role and a candidate.

The human resource challenge, while critical at the senior management levels, begins with retaining people over time in an organization. Salamon (2002) noted that the retention rate in nonprofit organizations has declined over time at all levels (p. 22). There can be no long-term development of future leaders if people do not stay in the organization. A plan for staff development can increase organizational effectiveness while motivating the best and brightest to stay in the organization. These plans need to begin within the nonprofit sector itself (Eisenberg, 2004, para 18; Hailey & James, 2004, p. 351).

Another challenge faced by nonprofit organizations revolves around the implementation of good management practices that result in organizations that function more effectively. Gelatt (1992) illustrated the lack of sound management practices in nonprofit organizations by listing ten problems faced by every nonprofit executive (pp. ix-xiii). These included lack of long-range planning, ineffective financial record-keeping practices, poor communication internally and with external constituency, and lack of clear parameters for the governing board. Gelatt's contribution to these challenges was a text aimed at addressing the gap that existed at that time between best business practice and the management practices of nonprofits. Many of the challenges noted above are tied to management practices that were addressed by Gelatt. His desire was to aid nonprofits in developing a clear sense of mission and to be well-led and well-managed through good management practices (p. xv).

The nonprofit sector also faces challenges apart from leadership and management. Salamon (2002) has cited new fiscal realities, the emergence of new technologies, increasing competition from the for-profit sector, and a new level of accountability from stakeholders as challenges facing nonprofits (pp. 12-22). These challenges affect all aspects of the nonprofit operation. Meeting these challenges requires the work of leaders with a wide range of competencies. How well these challenges are met will determine the level of public support and goodwill nonprofit organizations will have in the coming years.

These organizational challenges are only part of the equation. Nonprofits also face increasing demand for the services they provide. The segments of society that historically have relied on a variety of nonprofit organizations are increasing in size. The elderly population has doubled between 1960 and 2000. By 2025, there will be four times as many elderly as there were in 1960. There are an increasing number of refugees, women in the workforce, out-of-wedlock births, and children requiring foster care for a variety of reasons (Salamon, 2002, p. 23). These demographic changes result in greater demand for services at a time when nonprofit organizations face challenges related to funding and having enough trained personnel to operate.

All these challenges currently faced by nonprofit organizations must be addressed, and those in leadership roles bear the greater portion of this burden. If nonprofit organizations are to meet these challenges and continue to accomplish their important service to society, they will need leaders with the competencies to rally individuals as donors and as volunteers. Leaders will need to develop organizational structures and plans that will allow people to know that their investment is being used wisely and effectively in meeting the needs of society. The process of finding or developing these types of leaders can be enabled by using a competency model that identifies what is needed and then matches the leadership needs with the competencies of the individual.

The Role of the Nonprofit Leader

The focus of this literature review now shifts from looking at the history, characteristics, and contributions of the nonprofit sector to looking at the role of the nonprofit leader. This section reviews literature that pertains to the role of the nonprofit leader with specific attention given to the executive leader. A limited but growing amount of literature focuses on nonprofit leaders.

Roles Specific to Nonprofit Leaders

While there is a large body of work on leadership in general, the work by Nanus and Dobbs (1999) is notable in that it was written specifically with the nonprofit executive leader in mind. Nanus and Dobbs recognized that leadership within the nonprofit sector was different from leadership in the for-profit sector in a number of ways. These differences included that much of the work within nonprofits is done by volunteers; that success of the nonprofit is measured in terms of the social good it contributes; and finally, that the relationship between the leader and the board does not fit the usual pattern found in the for-profit arena (pp. 11-12). In addition, Drucker (1990) noted that nonprofit organizations need to be concerned with the challenges of fundraising, changes in organizations often run by volunteers, keeping their best people from burning out because of their intense commitment, and relating to various constituencies (p. xv).

A trend in nonprofit organizations striving for professionalization is illustrated by the use of management techniques such as strategic planning, financial analysis, public relations, and computerized databases. This striving for professionalization or adoption of management practices pioneered in the business sector is due in part to the need for greater efficiency demanded by stakeholders asking for demonstrable success of stated outcomes (Nanus & Dobbs, 1999, p. 47; Salamon, 2002, pp. 38-39). The concern for demonstrable success in nonprofit organization has contributed to the adoption of management techniques used by for-profit organizations. Nonprofit leaders must learn to adopt the techniques, but not at the expense of their particular organization's mission. Some may question this professionalization; however, building an organization that is responsive to the needs of its constituency while being highly innovative will require new ways of doing things (p. 50).

Nanus and Dobbs (1999) noted that leaders in nonprofit organizations must give their attention to four directions simultaneously, illustrated in the quadrant diagram seen in Figure 1.

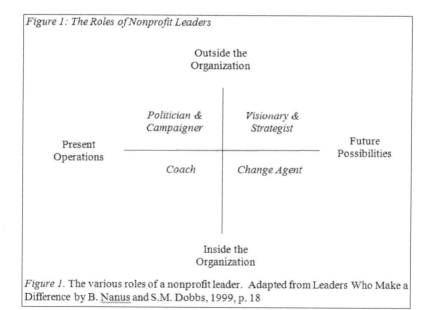

Figure 1: The Roles of Nonprofit Leaders

Outside the Organization

Politician & Campaigner

Visionary & Strategist

Present Operations

Future Possibilities

Coach

Change Agent

Inside the Organization

Figure 1. The various roles of a nonprofit leader. Adapted from Leaders Who Make a Difference by B. Nanus and S.M. Dobbs, 1999, p. 18

In Figure 1, the vertical axis represents a continuum of internal versus external focus for the nonprofit leader. The leader must understand not only the external constituency and needs, but also how well the organization is placed to address the needs that fall within the mission of the organization. The horizontal axis of the quadrant model highlights the ability of the leader to give attention to the present operation of the organization while maintaining a forward focus (Nanus & Dobbs, 1999, p. 18). While an organization may effectively serve its constituency today, it must also prepare to meet the future needs.

To effectively maintain progress on these fronts, Nanus and Dobbs (1999) have suggested that six distinct roles emerge that are critical to the success of the nonprofit leader. They include:

1. The leader as a visionary—The leader needs to identify the direction in which the organization should move. An effective vision will be compelling and clearly communicated.

2. The leader as a strategist—Not only should the leader possess the ability to identify and communicate a vision, she or he needs the skills necessary to develop and implement the strategies needed to make the vision a reality.

3. The leader as a politician—The leader is the spokesperson, advocate and chief negotiator of the organization. The leader becomes the public face and often the only person the public will connect with the organization.

4. The leader as a campaigner—The leader not only presents the vision to the public in a positive light, he or she also must be adept at fundraising and enlisting other types of support. Most nonprofits do not generate enough income through their operations, so funds must be raised to sustain them.

5. The leader as a coach—Nonprofits are like any other organization, they do not function without people. The leader must see to the recruiting, training and empowering of people so that the organization's constituency is well served.

6. The leader as a change agent—For any organization to move effectively into the future, some type of change must be involved. Leaders of nonprofits must be constantly aware of new opportunities and needs within their constituency and then take steps to meet the needs that fall within the mandate of the organization. (pp. 17-19)

Nanus and Dobbs acknowledged the complexity of the leadership task in keeping the four distinct aspects of leadership in balance. Significant failure in understanding the present reality of the organization and its future direction, coupled with lack of attention to the conditions inside or outside the organization, will lead to organizational ineffectiveness. The six roles outlined provide a roadmap to allow nonprofit leaders to think and act more deliberately as they lead in this complex environment. The intent is not to create a single model for all nonprofits regardless of the context, but rather to consider the complexity of the leadership role and the skill set necessary to lead a nonprofit organization successfully.

One of the most prolific writers in the field of leadership and management in recent history focused on the role of the nonprofit leader. Drucker (1990) wrote that the leader of the nonprofit organization must give attention to a few important items as part of the leadership role. These included the fit between the leader and the organization, the ability and willingness to listen well, and commitment to the task of leading the organization (pp. 19-20). The leader of a nonprofit also must balance the long-range plan with the more immediate needs. The leader must give attention to a wide range of organizational concerns while ensuring that the details necessary for the efficient operation of the organization are in place (p. 23).

Attracting individuals with a great deal of talent and ability is another important role for a leader. The performance and future of the organization depends on those who join the organization in a variety of roles. The leader's ability to attract and retain quality people is an important measure of leadership success (p. 26). The role of the nonprofit leader must also include taking time to communicate with those who are stakeholders in the organization. This may be a time-consuming process, but it is necessary.

Fleishman (2007), when he referred to his experience with leaders from various foundations, noted there was no such thing as "the very model of a modern foundation president" (p. 228). Fleishman specifically mentioned that the best foundation presidents all possessed the ability to refrain from dwelling on their own personal importance. They were able to resist the lure of being seduced by the power that comes with giving away vast sums of money (p. 229). This observation concurred with Collins' (2001) finding that the best leaders also possess a compelling modesty related to their own contributions to the success of the organization (p. 27).

There are competing perspectives in leadership literature regarding the difference or lack of difference between leading a nonprofit and leading a business. Even though Drucker noted that management is the same regardless of varying organizational purposes (Drucker, 1994, p. 72), he also pointed out that nonprofits have distinctive needs in the area of leadership and management (Drucker, 1990, p. xv). On the other hand, studies have been conducted that show that what people desire from leaders during a crisis varies little from a nonprofit setting to a business setting (Peterson & Van Fleet , 2008, p. 514; Smith, 2000, p. 183). This variation in perspectives illustrates the complexity of gaining a clear understanding of how the role of a nonprofit leader may or may not vary from their counterpart in the business or public sector. The lack of a well-formed body of literature has meant that, in the absence of empirical research, speculation and "borrowing" from other sectors have occurred to fill the void.

Servant-Leadership and the Nonprofit Leader

Borrowing from other sectors can generate helpful insights into the role of the nonprofit leader and the practice of management in nonprofits. One place to look for insights into the role and function of a nonprofit leader would be in literature that outlined servant leadership. A focus on the needs and aspirations of others, the hallmark of most nonprofit organizations, lies at the very heart of servant-leadership as it was originally articulated by Robert Greenleaf. Greenleaf (1995) observed that the servant-leader is first a servant and then a leader. The reverse, being leader first and servant second, may be the stance of some leaders, but likely is derived from the need for power or material possessions and is usually unhealthy for followers (p. 22). The distinction between the individual who places service ahead of leadership is that the servant-leader ensures that "other people's highest priority needs are being served" (p. 22). Putting other people's priorities first is evidenced by growth that takes place in the lives of individuals. Greenleaf explained that when people are being well served, they become healthier, wiser, freer, and more autonomous, and likely are capable of serving others (p. 22).

Other individuals have added to the literature on servant-leadership since Greenleaf introduced the concept. Larry Spears (2002) has promoted servant-leadership as a pattern for leaders in all types of organizations. Spears noted that a great deal of attention has been given to the character and character traits of leaders in recent years (para. 2). He also asserted, "Servant-leadership truly offers hope and guidance for a new era in human development, and for the creation of better, more caring institutions" (2004, p. 11). Servant-leadership can make a valuable contribution to the work of Nanus and Dobbs by adding leader characteristics to a model that focuses mainly on the roles of the leader.

Spears (2002) noted ten characteristics viewed as being central to the development and practice of servant-leadership. They are as follows:

1. Listening—The leader listens receptively to what is being said by others. Listening, coupled with periods of reflection, is essential.

2. Empathy—The leader assumes that individuals have the best intentions, even though the leader may need to refuse to accept certain behaviors or actions.

3. Healing—This characteristic refers to the recognition that many individuals have emotional hurts. The healing of relationships and bringing of wholeness is a powerful aspect of servant-leadership.

4. Awareness—This characteristic encompasses not only self-awareness, but also awareness of the context and issues. It leads to having an integrated and holistic perspective on a given situation.

5. Persuasion—Servant-leaders seek to convince rather than coerce others. They seek to build consensus in place of imposing their will on their followers.

6. Conceptualization—Spears noted that "servant-leaders seek to nurture their abilities to dream great dreams" (Ten Characteristics section, para. 7). The ability to see the possibilities and look beyond the daily operation is an essential quality for a leader to possess.

7. Foresight—This is closely related to conceptual-ization, but differs in that it takes into consideration

the past and the present, and sees a potential outcome related to a current reality. It is deeply rooted in one's intuitive mind.

8. Stewardship—Stewards hold something in trust for another. In this case, the servant-leader holds the organization in trust for the greater good of society. The outcomes of the organization ought to make a positive difference in the lives of those being served.

9. Commitment to the growth of people—Servant-leaders recognize the intrinsic value of the individual apart from what he or she contributes to the organization. This belief causes the leaders to seek the personal development of each individual within the organization, not only for the benefit of the organization, but more importantly, for their own benefit.

10. Building community—This aspect of servant-leadership assumes that people function best when in a community, and that community can be created within an organization. It is within community that individuals are developed, cared for, and given a sense of belonging (Ten Characteristics section).

This list of characteristics is not intended to be exhaustive, but rather to show the promise and power of servant-leadership (Ten Characteristics, para. 13). Spears argued that if these characteristics were true of leaders, regardless of the type of organization, the workplace would be much healthier, happy, and productive.

The Both/And for Nonprofit Leaders

A comparison of the characteristics outlined by Spears for servant-leadership and the roles articulated by Nanus and Dobbs for nonprofit leaders reveals distinct areas of emphasis, with some similarities and overlap. The roles articulated by Nanus and Dobbs (1999) focus largely on the activities and actions of the nonprofit leader. Spears (2002, 2004) approached leadership with the servant-leadership model in mind and therefore focused on the characteristics of a servant-leader rather than the roles. Spear's intent was to create a picture of the personal characteristics necessary for the practice of servant-leadership. While characteristics will lead to a certain set of actions, Spears does not seek to prescribe the jobs, tasks, or roles that the leader must complete. Rather, he is portraying the attitudes and perspectives of an individual who practices servant-leadership. Spears' list is very much about the person of the leader and the results that can brought about in an organization.

Although servant-leadership places an emphasis on the person of the leader by noting certain qualities and abilities that ought to be true of the servant-leader, the roles articulated by Nanus and Dobbs (1999) are less about the person of the leader and more about the skill set or the most critical responsibilities of a leader. These roles highlight the critical tasks that a leader must perform to ensure that the purpose is accomplished in the nonprofit organization. The focus is very much on "doing," with little said about the "person" of the leader apart from tasks or roles. In contrast, many of the leadership characteristics noted by Spears as the hallmark of a servant-leader are strongly supported and driven by the personal values of the leader. It would be difficult for a leader to display the characteristics identified by Spears without having a certain level of personal maturity, self-awareness, and a sense of value ascribed to the individuals in the organization. These are the kinds of characteristics and values that can be brought to light through the use of a competency model.

Leadership Competency

Much has been written on the subject of leadership competency in books and journal articles. However, care must be taken to gain a proper understanding of the intended context and the meaning of the authors when they speak of leadership competence. There are a variety of perspectives regarding what constitute the "competencies" of a leader. This confusion regarding competency stems from various ideas regarding the definition of competency and is further complicated by the variety of contexts in which leaders operate. Competencies are contextually bound, and having proper understanding of the context in which a leader is functioning is pivotal to leadership success (Barner, 2000; Zigarmi, Lyles, & Fowler, 2005). It is not a matter of discerning which of the ideas about the competency or roles of the leaders is right or wrong; rather, it is a matter of understanding how they fit together and contribute to the formation of a broader and richer picture of leadership. This study looked at the role of the executive leader in a nonprofit organization.

The Beginnings of the Competency Movement

The first mention of competence used to describe characteristics associated with superior performance was attributed to Robert W. White in a 1959 journal article (Le Deist & Winterton, 2005, p. 31). In this article, entitled "Motivation Reconsidered: The Concept of Competence," White proposed a connection between cognitive competence and motivational action tendencies. White defined competence as an "organism's capacity to interact effectively with its environment" (White, 1959, p. 297). White viewed people as being highly capable of developing greater levels of competence and wanted to understand the motivational aspects of competence development. White's work opened the door for the study of competence as an aspect of human development related to performance in the workplace. White's initial work focused largely on child development, and in this context "effectiveness" was not clearly defined. In later research on competence, particularly as it related to the workplace, definitions of success or effectiveness were necessary.

Another important factor in the development of competency testing is the North American fascination with measurement and prediction that found expression in the wave of testing that emerged in the post-war era of the 1950s. Intelligence and aptitude testing were widely used in the United States by the 1960s and 1970s. Standardized testing was used in most schools, and entrance exams such as the Scholastic Aptitude Test (SAT) were the norm for all students wishing to pursue higher education. McClelland challenged this use of intelligence testing and proposed an alternative. The alternative suggested was that a new way of testing be developed that would test for competence, not intelligence (p.7).

McClelland (1973) went on to suggest six characteristics of competency testing. They were as follows:

1. The best testing is criterion sampling—the implication is that if you want to determine what it takes to be successful in a given occupation or role, you need to base your assessment for predicting success on the known activity of those already deemed successful in the field.

2. Tests should be designed to reflect the changes in what the individual has learned—based on the criterion sampling established, one should be able to measure changes (an increase) in one's ability to perform a given task related to the criterion.

3. How to improve on the characteristics tested should be made public and explicit—when the criterion upon which an individual will be tested is known, the individual then is able to improve his or her skills in that area. The criterion must be related to skills or characteristics needed in real-life situations for the testing to have a purpose.

4. Tests should assess competencies involved in clusters of life outcomes—the actual number of skills or activities required for a given job would be quite numerous. It may be advantageous to group similar competencies for ease of assessment.

5. Tests should involve operant as well as respondent behavior—tests often measure respondent behavior based on a highly structured test environment. Real life is not that highly structured and requires testing that allows for choosing alternatives that are not clearly defined.

6. Tests should sample operant thought patterns to get maximum generalizability to various action outcomes—the tests ought not to measure only the actions themselves, but ought also to define the thought patterns associated with successful actions.

McClelland (1973) desired to create a testing method that would not just measure intelligence, which was not an accurate predictor of success in life, but rather would develop a means of actually assessing the various competencies present in an individual that would lead to vocational success (p. 13). It has also been noted that traditional assessment methods are biased against minorities, women, and persons from lower socioeconomic strata (Fallows, 1985, p. 1; McClelland, 1973).

Leadership Competency Defined

A significant challenge in dealing with the notion of leadership competency is finding a widely accepted definition of the concept. White's (1959) definition of competence as "an organism's capacity to interact effectively with its environment" is one of the earliest found in print, but has never been widely used in connection with leadership competence. This earliest of definition is an example of behavioristic thinking. McClelland

(1973) wrote of competency, but did so without giving any explicit definition. He did, however, refer to competence as the abilities required to complete a given job successfully (pp. 6-7). McClelland's reference to White in *Testing for Competence* is very general and does not attempt to define competence in light of White's work linking competence and motivation. Since McClelland's work came out, competency has been defined and used in a variety of ways. In one of the earliest books on competency, Boyatzis (1983) defined a job competence as an "underlying characteristic of a person in that it may be a motive, trait, skill, aspect of one's self-image or social role, or a body of knowledge which he or she uses" (p. 21).

Boyatzis further noted that competencies may not be consciously known to the individual, in that the person may not be able to articulate or describe the competency itself. A given competency may be evident only when the actions of the individual are evaluated to discern the motives and thought processes undertaken in a particular situation. In this early work, Boyatzis framed the discussion of individual competencies as an integral part of job performance (p. 12). He suggested that individual competencies, along with the demands of that particular job and the organizational environment, were related factors in determining whether the action taken by the individual would be deemed effective. Action taken in one environment may not be appropriate or effective in another. Likewise, actions taken in the performance of one role may not be effective, but when taken in the context of another job or role, they would be viewed as very effective. This relationship is illustrated in Figure 2.

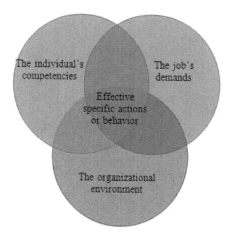

Figure 2: A Model of Effective Jobs performance

The individual's competencies

The job's demands

Effective specific actions or behavior

The organizational environment

Figure 2. Boyatzis' model showing the relationship between job demands, competence and environment. Adapted from *The Competent Manager* by R.E. Boyatzis, 1983, p. 13.

This figure serves to illustrate the complexity of assessing leadership effectiveness (Boyatzis, 1983, p. 13). Effective action and the resulting performance are the product of all three components. While the most desirable situation for a leader is present when all three components are aligned, Boyatzis noted that "if any two of the components are consistent, or congruent, then there is an increased likelihood that effective performance will occur" (p. 14). The point is that effective performance in any given role is not simply a matter of the individual's having the appropriate skill set; the skill set must be used in the proper role within the right context for the greatest level of effectiveness to exist.

Even though Boyatzis did not describe it as such, this is an example of a "system." Haines (1999) identified a system as a group of interacting, interrelated, or interdependent components that form a unified whole. The components could be physical objects or in this case intangibles such as values, beliefs, characteristics, organizational environment, or job demands (p. 2). Changes in any one of these components will have an effect on the others. Leadership competencies that reside in the individual must be viewed within the framework of a wider "system" that includes the context of a given role. In assessing competence for any role, the context and the expectations of that role must also be considered.

Part of the "system" for leaders would be the leader themselves. The values, perspectives, motivations, and character of a person are as much a part of the leadership equation as what a person knows and what they do. We lead from who we are because who we are influences our actions, what we do and how we do it. This point was emphasized by Lowney (2003) when writing on the Jesuit order. The longevity and effectives of the Society of Jesus can be attributed at least in part, according to Lowney, to the fact that they understood that leadership sprang from within, and therefore required a high degree of self-awareness (p. 15). A high degree of self-awareness allows the individual to most effectively conduct themselves in any given situation. This is an important skill for a leader or manager in a changing and complex environment.

The value of the model proposed by Boyatzis (1983) can be summarized by the following quotation:

The job demands component reveals primarily *what* a person in the job is expected to do. The organizational environment component reveals some aspects of what a person in a management job is expected to do, but primarily reveals *how* a person is expected to respond to the job demands. The individual's competencies component reveals what a person is capable of doing; it reveals *why* he or she may act in certain ways. (p. 16)

A missing component in many definitions of competency is the personal characteristics or values that provide the motivation for action. If we truly lead from who we are as suggested by Lowney, then Boyatzis was correct in asserting that competency must also consider why individuals act in particular ways. The intangible side of leadership truly does matter.

The work of Boyatzis is significant to the discussion of competency because not only did he frame competency within a broader organizational context and brings forward the notion of personal motivation, as noted above, but he also introduced the idea that there are different types and levels of competency as part of the model. Based on research conducted using the Job Competence Assessment Method, Boyatzis (1983) developed a list of 21 characteristics of a competent manager. Two criteria were considered in the development of this list. First, the characteristic had to distinguish effective performance in a management role in a statistically significant manner; and second, the characteristic could not be unique to a particular product or service (Boyatzis, 1983, p. 26). The resulting list included 21 types of characteristics (listed in alphabetical order): (a) accurate self-assessment; (b) conceptualization; (c) concern with close relationships; (d) concern with impact; (e) developing others; (f) diagnostic use of concepts; (g) efficiency orientation; (h) logical thought; (i) managing group process; (j) memory; (k) perceptual objectivity; (l) positive regard; (m) proactivity; (n) self-confidence; (o) self-control; (p) specialized knowledge; (q) spontaneity; (r) stamina and adaptability; (s) use or [*sic*] oral presentations; (t) use of socialized power; and (u) use of unilateral power (p. 26).

Boyatzis (1983) noted that a competency model should describe levels for each of the competencies (p. 27). The competencies could exist at different levels within the individual. The three levels proposed by Boyatzis are motives and traits at the

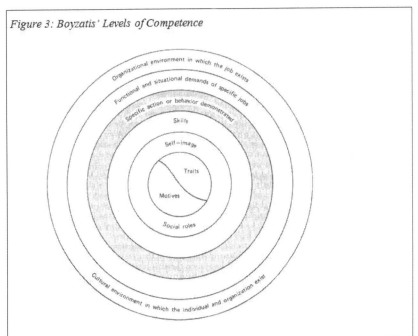

Figure 3: Boyzatis' Levels of Competence

Organizational environment in which the job exists

Functional and situational demands of specific jobs

Specific action or behavior demonstrated

Skills

Self-image

Traits

Motives

Social roles

Cultural environment in which the individual and organization exist

Figure 3. The three levels at which competencies can be found and their relationship to environment. Adapted from *The Competent Manager* by R.E. Boyzatis, 1983, p. 34.

unconscious level, self-image and social role at the conscious level, and skills at the behavioral level (Boyatzis, 1983, p. 27). Boyatzis viewed these three levels of competency not only as interrelated with one another, but also as foundational for the actions and behavior of the individual within a given role and environment. Figure 3 (above) illustrates this dynamic interaction.

The interactions between a person and his or her environment results in some type of action or behavior's occurring (Boyatzis, 1983, p. 34). Fcedback takes place continuously between the competency level (the inner three levels) and the outer two levels (environment and the specific job) as they meet at the action or behavior level. If the actions that are a result of the competencies are a good fit with the outer two levels, then the feedback will be positive. If, however, the action or behavior is perceived as negative, then the feedback will also be negative.

Negative feedback provides an opportunity to determine what adjustments might be made to ensure better performance. The possibility of changes in the environment and the functional demands of the rolc or adjustments to the individual competencies are all options to consider. This understanding of alignment of individual competencies with the role and the environment is evidenced in Collins' (2001) work when he refers to having the right people on the bus, but also having them in the right seats on the bus. This distinction illustrates that individual competency is not a guarantee of success. The individual must have the proper role (right seat) in the right environment (the bus) for top performance to be evoked. Collins went on to say that to keep someone who does not fit in a particular role does not show respect for the individual or for the organization. At times, the best course of action is to release someone to pursue a role in an environment that is a better fit for him or her (p. 53).

Spencer and Spencer had a very similar but more developed definition of competency. They write, "A competency is an *underlying characteristic* of an individual that is *causally related* to *criterion-referenced effective and/or superior performance* in a job situation" (Spencer & Spencer, 1993, p. 9; emphasis in original). This definition represents the further development in the understanding and function of competency within the work environment.

It is important to understand the implications of certain parts of this definition. The words "underlying characteristic" mean that the competency is rooted deeply in the motives or traits of the individual. The phrase "causally related" implies that the presence of a particular competency causes or predicts behavior that leads to achieving a particular level of performance (Spencer & Spencer, 1993, p. 12). If the competency cannot be tied to specific action, then it is not a competency and is merely a characteristic or a trait. When a competency is "criterion-referenced," it means that the competency can actually predict who will do something well (p. 13). According to Spencer and Spencer, a competency must predict something that is meaningful in the real world. They explained that "a characteristic or credential that makes no difference in performance is not a competency and should not be used to evaluate people" (p. 13).

The idea that individual competencies are the foundation of individual performance, which leads to organizational effectiveness, has been studied by others. Soosay (2005) demonstrated that the foundation of continuous innovation in a logistics management firm is the competence of the individuals in the firm (p. 300). The extent to which an organization is able to recognize and nurture individual competencies will have a significant impact on the organization's effectiveness in accomplishing its purpose (Doyle, 1995, p. 29). It is imperative, then, that organizations give attention to the competencies of their staff not only when doing further training, but also in the hiring process.

The model of competency proposed by Spencer and Spencer breaks the types of competencies into five categories, as opposed to the three levels of Boyatzis. When analyzed, the differences between the two models are minimal. Spencer and Spencer (1993) noted five types of competency characteristics: motives, traits, self-concept, knowledge, and skill (pp. 9-11).

Spencer and Spencer used a diagram of an iceberg to illustrate another aspect of the proposed competency levels or types. The iceberg model showed the distinction between the hidden and the visible elements of competency. The visible elements are skill and knowledge, while the hidden elements are self-concept, traits, and motives. Spencer and Spencer (1993) contended that the core personality competencies, the hidden aspects of trait and motive, are not only the most difficult to see, but are also the most difficult to develop and change (p. 11). These deeply held aspects of competency change only with a great deal of effort on the part of the individual. Spencer and Spencer observed that the aspects of skill and knowledge were most easily developed, in part because they are more easily observed.

This understanding of personal change is supported by the work of Hargrove (1995) where he referred to single, double, and triple loop learning in the individual change process. Triple-Loop learning is seeing transformation by creating a shift in person's context or point of view about himself or herself. There is a fundamental shift in the individual's values, touching on motives. Double-Loop learning entails reshaping the underlying patterns of people's thinking and behavior so they are capable of doing different things. This change does not go as deep as triple-loop learning, but the change in behavior ought to be transferable to other similar situations. Single-Loop learning focuses on helping people embody new skills and capabilities through incremental improvement. This is the most basic level, and normally the individual is not able to transfer the learning to another task (p. 27).

Another significant aspect of competency as defined by Spencer and Spencer relates to the authors' portrayal of the causal relationships of the levels or types of competencies. This causal relationship is described as the job performance or outcome flowing from the behavior of the individual, which is the result of the individual's personal characteristics. These personal characteristics are motives, traits, self-concept, and knowledge, which provide the basis for action or behavior (Spencer & Spencer, 1993, pp. 12-13). In this way, competencies are linked to outcomes or job performance. If, as noted, competencies are not linked to performance, then they are not considered a competency.

Criteria referencing is another characteristic of competency studies. Spencer and Spencer (1993) cited two levels of criteria: *superior performance* and *effective performance* (p. 13). Statistically, superior performance is defined as being "one standard deviation above average" and amounts to about 1 person in 10 in a given working situation (p. 13). Effective performance denotes "minimally acceptable" results in the workplace (p. 13). An individual who does not function at even the minimal level of effectiveness level would not be considered competent for that particular role. At that point, it would be necessary to evaluate whether the shortfall is due to a wrong placement of the individual, or whether development of latent competencies is required.

Spencer and Spencer (1993) presented two categories of competencies in relation to the job performance criterion that they predict (p. 15). The two categories are *threshold competencies* and *differentiating competencies*. Threshold competencies are described as basic skills or essential characteristics that anyone would need to be successful in a given role.

Differentiating competencies are factors that are evident in those who attain a superior level of performance and are not present in the same manner in those who achieve only an average level of performance (Spencer & Spencer, 1993, p. 15). It may not be the case that the competency is absent in those who attain average performance; it could be the case that the competency is not expressed at the same level or with similar proficiency as someone who excels in a particular role.

The Development of Competency Measures

The development of instruments and methods of assessing competency provided the foundation upon which the competency movement was built. One of the testing methods employed in an endeavor to identify competencies was a form of the critical-incident technique (CIT) as developed by Flanagan (1954). CIT was a method developed to collect direct observations of human behavior that would allow the data to be used to solve some type of defined problem. CIT outlined procedures and criteria that would make this possible (Dubois & Rothwell, 2004, pp. 16-17). The CIT was refined to become the Behavioral-Event Interview (BEI) (Boyatzis, 1983, p. 41; McClelland, 1998, p. 331). BEI became step three of a five-step Job Competence Assessment Method developed by McBer & Company to generate a validated competence model for a particular role (Boyatzis, 1983, p. 41). BEI incorporated McClelland's six characteristics of competency testing to establish a method of assessing an individual's competence based on his or her own previous experience. McClelland(1998) observed that the success of executive level leaders is seldom indicated by success on intelligence tests (p. 331). He noted that occupational success was able to be better predicted when testing was based on competencies rather than on intelligence tests (p. 331). However, the downside of the BEI is that it is labor and time intensive and therefore expensive, as well as being individually focused. There have been attempts to develop competency tests that could be used with wider samples of individuals, but to date these have not gained the acceptance achieved by BEI (p. 331).

The purpose of the BEI was to allow for flexibility in discovering the difference between those who have been identified as being outstanding at a particular job (O group) and those who have been identified at a lesser rate as being outstanding in the same role (T group) (McClelland, 1998, p. 332). McClelland noted that this approach is used because "people agree more readily on who is outstanding than on what makes them outstanding" (p. 332). The intended outcomes of the BEI are to develop a list of competencies that are unique to, or are present in a greater measure in, the O group than in the T group. Using this methodology, the researcher is able to determine the competencies present in those who have a higher level of performance.

One of the first uses McClelland found for this new approach to job effectiveness was with the U.S. State Department in the 1970s. The U.S. Information Service (USIS) had found that high scores of applicants on the Foreign Services Information Officers (FSIO) exam did not necessarily predict success as with an FSIO (Spencer, McClelland, & Spencer, 1994, p. 4). It was this opportunity to find an alternative to traditional assessment measures that would predict job performance that led to some of the first published studies using BEI. This method differs from others in that traditional job analysis looks at elements of the job, while competency assessment studies the people who do the job well and then defines the competencies in terms of the characteristics and behaviors of these people (p. 5).

From the beginning of the competency movement as outlined in this review, the study, development, and application of competency models can be seen in many organizations identified as "best-practice" organizations when it comes to leadership development (Fulmer & Wagner, 1999, p. 30). The research carried out has led to the development of "competency dictionaries" that catalogue and define generic competencies. The individual competencies have been used to create more than 300 BEI-based competency models for jobs in a variety of industries that span the globe (Boyatzis, 1983; Spencer, McClelland, & Spencer, 1994, p. 19).

Benefits and Limitations of Competency Models

The benefits to organizations of knowing the characteristics or competencies of higher performing individuals are multiple. McClelland (1998) noted two specific examples of benefit to the organization from a study that explored the value of using a competency model in hiring senior leaders. The first is that executives who received feedback on competencies combined with setting goals for change related to their competencies showed improvement when measured two years later (p. 336). This result illustrates the power of specific feedback on the performance of individuals. Accurate and timely input can lead to a higher level of performance on the part of individuals.

The second area of benefit for organizations that use a competency model involves the recruitment process. One of the main reasons the study was undertaken was to deal with the issue of costly executive turnover (McClelland, 1998, p. 336). It was estimated that 17 of 35 executives hired in 1992 using conventional methods had left the company by 1994. Due to various factors, the executives that left cost the company at least $4 million (p. 336).

This type of turnover is not only expensive from a recruitment standpoint, but it also hampers the productivity of the division in which these executives served, and, in turn, of the company as a whole. It is difficult to sustain continuity with constant changes in executive-level leadership.

In contrast, of the 32 executives hired using competency measures developed from the BEI, only two had left the company in the next 24 months. This was a 6.3% turnover rate versus 49% from the previous executive cohort. The estimated saving was $3.5 million (McClelland, 1998, p. 336). The unquantifiable advantages of this reduced turnover included sustaining productivity, momentum, and morale, all of which may be adversely affected by the change of executive level leadership within a given division or area of a company. Being able to predict success and improve effectiveness of those in leadership using competency measures is of benefit to the individuals themselves and to the company. While the method used in this particular study was able to predict executive success, it also indicated that more research is needed to explore questions raised by the results (p. 338). This study supports the conclusions of Spencer and Spencer (1993), who wrote, "Competency-based selection predicts superior job performance and retention—both with significant economic value to the organization—without race, age, gender, or demographic bias" (p. 8).

The idea of using leadership competencies in an organization has been the subject of both praise and caution. Jay Conger and Douglas Ready (2004) highlighted the positive aspects of a competency model as bringing clarity, consistency, and connectivity to the task of leadership development within an organization. They do, also point out, however, that competency models have their downside, including being complicated, conceptual, and built around current realities (p. 44). Leadership competencies derived from the performance of leaders in 2010 may not be appropriate for the next generation of leaders (p. 46). The most effective uses of competency models in leadership development must be considered not only in terms of the behavioral aspect but also in terms of the business strategy and its implications for the leadership needs of the organization (Barner, 2000, p. 48; Zemke & Zemke, 1999, pp. 70-71).

The competencies required of leaders will also vary from one organization to another, depending on business plans and goals. Barner (2000) observed, "It makes no sense to try and identify essential leadership capabilities unless one knows the business context in which the leader will be expected to excel" (p. 47). This approach will result in great variance in what are viewed as the competencies required by top level leaders. This result is evidenced by the competencies identified by various organizations in the literature. Eli Lilly seeks to have potential leaders model seven leadership behaviors (Conger & Ready, 2004, p. 42), while RBC Financial Group, in response to their desire to "execute their strategic imperative and most important core values," articulated four behaviors deemed necessary for leaders of RBC in an environment where cross-border acquisitions were necessary (p. 42). These four behaviors became the map for leadership development at RBC. The qualities and behaviors articulated were explicitly tied to the outcomes desired. Conger and Ready cited both Eli Lilly and RBC as examples of companies that used competency models not only for the development of leaders, but also for the assessment of individual leadership potential.

Drucker (1998) claimed that the differences between managing a software company, a hospital, a church, or the Boy Scouts amounted to no more than 10% of the work done. This 10% was a difference in strategy and structure that is brought on by the difference in mission ("The Discipline of Management," paras. 14-16). These statements imply that the tasks of leaders are remarkably similar in all types of organizations and that the chief differences are rooted in the specific mission. This situation will lead to variance in the required competencies in a given organization, but also provides a basis for understanding that a core set of leadership competencies are needed by leaders in any organization.

Leadership Competency in Broader Literature
While Boyatzis and Spencer and Spencer are representative of how competency has been defined and understood by American researchers in the last 20 years, there remains a great deal of confusion regarding what the term *competency* implies in other settings and places. This can be attributed in part to how terminology is used when referring to the leadership and management roles within an organization. The term "roles" is used when referring only to the specific actions or expectations of those in leadership. The term "role" most often references the leader's actions and not his or her competencies. An

example of this usage can be found in the writings of Henry Mintzberg.

In one seminal piece written on leadership or management roles Mintzberg (1975) identified ten roles that are critical to the success of managers and leaders. While the label of "competency" was not used, what Mintzberg described was a set of "organized sets of behaviors identified with a position" (p. 54). Mintzberg's intention was not to deal with competencies underlying those behaviors, but rather with the behaviors themselves. While the ten roles identified are very helpful in understanding what leaders or managers do, the characteristics or traits of those who successfully perform these roles is not addressed by Mintzberg. This is one of the weaknesses of discussing only the roles or behaviors of leaders without considering the underlying characteristics that lead to the behaviors or fulfilling the roles viewed as key. It is the competencies supporting the activity or roles that determine the actions and therefore are the leverage point for in assessment and development of staff. Roles indicate what people must do, but it is the competencies that focus on the individual's ability to fulfill those roles.

The literature examined contained many definitions associated with the concept of competence or competency. Le Deist and Winterton (2005) indicated that the term "competence" generally refers to functional areas, while "competency" is most often used in reference to behavioral areas (p. 27). The basis for this claim is not clarified, but the authors indicated that this understanding of the terminology is not consistent throughout the literature. Indeed, there are a wide variety of definitions associated with competence and competency. Terms such as qualities, skills, abilities, knowledge, talents, and behaviors have been used by a number of authors in describing competency (Davis, Naughton, & Rothwell, 2004, p. 28; Dubois & Rothwell, 2004, p. 16; Fulmer & Wagner, 1999, p. 31). Elkin (1990) supported the perspective of Le Deist and Winterton when he quoted Hammond, who observed that competencies are "not the tasks of the job, they are what enables people to do the tasks" (p. 21).

Other definitions of competency highlight the aspects of performance, behavior, and outcomes. The underlying characteristics, traits, or competencies lead to tangible outcomes deemed as indicators of success. An example of this aspect of competence is evident in the definition provided by Davis, Naughton, and Rothwell (2004) where they wrote: "Competencies include clusters of skills, knowledge, abilities, and behaviors required for people to succeed" (p. 28). Boyatzis (1983) linked competencies to actions or specific behavior used in the performance of a particular task (p. 21). Spencer and Spencer (1993) developed this notion further by suggesting that the result of competency is *criterion-referenced effective and/or superior performance* in a job or situation" (p. 9) (emphasis in original). These definitions imply that competency as commonly understood in the current literature is viewed as including the characteristics, traits, qualities, and skills of the individual that will lead to an action or measurable outcome that is deemed desirable. The study of competency focused on both aspects that are necessary for a complete understanding of competency. These examples show

how diversity is considered when referring to leadership competencies.

This vagueness and multiplicity of definitions of competency is also due to the word *competency* being used for different purposes in different settings. A study conducted by Boon and van der Klink (2002) found that the concept of competency "serves as a container with very flexible content" (p. 354). While this ambiguity might be frustrating on one level, the advantage is that it allows "competency" to be used to define a dynamic blend of knowledge, skills, attitudes, and motivation as they are investigated and applied to a variety of setting and roles. Due to the flexibility of the meaning of *competency*, dialogue between education and labor organizations can be enhanced as discussion takes place regarding what competence in the work place entails (p. 355). This particular study found that a competency framework is becoming more important due to the rapid change and uncertainty in the workforce. It was the suggestion of Boon and van der Klink that due to a lack of "precise professional requirements," competency would become a more important means of defining the necessary preparation for the workforce (p. 355). The researchers noted that a clear definition of competency is needed, but at the same time expressed concern regarding a comprehensive definition. One of these concerns is that the notion of competency is intrinsically linked to a given context, and a single definition may be restrictive. Boon and van der Klink also concluded that more study is needed to assess the advantages and disadvantages of using competency measures or models in various settings (p. 355).

The literature contains several definitions and usages of *competence* and *competency*. For the purpose of this study, *competency* will include motives, traits, self-concept, knowledge, and skills required for success in a given context. This definition includes the major elements noted in the literature and research related to competence and competency models.

The Development of Competency Models

A review of the relevant literature reveals a number of methods employed in the development of competency models in use as of 2010. Some, such as Critical Incident Interviewing, which led to the Behavioral Event Interviews, have a well-founded research methodology base from which researchers can draw conclusions regarding certain competencies (McClelland, 1998, p. 331). Other competency models are developed without the aid or benefit of rigorous research methods, resulting in models that are not thoroughly grounded. These are often developed by committees with a particular role in their organization in mind, resulting in a list of competencies that were questionable in terms of their usefulness beyond a very narrow window of application (Cockerill, Hunt, & Schroder, 1995, p. 6; Raven, 2001b, p. 121). This section will give an overview of some of the research methods used in the development of competency models.

As one of the key figures in the competency movement in the United States, McClelland has provided much insight and direction as the research base of competency movement developed. One method that emerged from Critical Incident Interview to be used in repeatedly in the development of competency models was the Behavioral Event Interview (BEI) (McClelland, 1998, p. 332; Raven, 2001b, p. 122). This methodology was developed by McClelland and colleagues at McBer and Company (Boyatzis, 1983, p. 41; Spencer & Spencer, 1993, p. 97) and has been widely used in the development and refinement of competency models for a variety of positions. This method moved beyond using two very different types of data that had been most commonly employed up to this point: The first was the external observer's ratings, and the second was the results of various personality tests that the subject filled out. The BEI allowed researchers to understand the connection between activity that was present in those deemed to be high performers and the motivation that drove that activity. The key was the link between activity and understanding the motivation behind the action. This distinguished BEI from the Critical Incident interview, in which questions were asked only about the activity itself and tangible outcomes.. Another distinguishing feature of the BEI was that the responses are coded for both frequency and the level of complexity or scope that is displayed (McClelland, 1998, p. 332).

The advantages and disadvantage of the BEI method were outlined by Spencer and Spencer (1993). They noted the advantages, as follows: It is possible to acquire empirical identification of competencies beyond or different from those generated by other data collection methods; the method is precise in terms of how competencies are expressed; it allows for identification of algorithms; it is free from racial, gender, and cultural biases; and it generates data for assessment training, and career pathing (p. 98).

The cumulative result of these advantages was a method of inquiry that allowed the researcher to gain an understanding not only of the actions of high performing individuals, but also of the motivations and attitudes that undergirded those behaviors. The data was also coded in a manner that allowed some measure of the intensity of a given competency in a particular setting, allowing for the development of models useful in the recruitment and training of others.

A number of weaknesses regarding the BEI methodology have been cited as well. These include the time and expense associated with carrying out the process, the expertise required of the interviewers and individuals coding the interviews, and the narrow focus of the interviews. The combination of these three challenges make BEI impractical for widespread, general use at multiple levels in all but the wealthiest of organizations (Spencer & Spencer, 1993, p. 99).

Because BEI was demanding in terms of cost and expertise, other models of establishing competency were developed that required less specialized training and fewer financial resources. Spencer and Spencer (1993) listed the alternative methods for use in competency studies as expert panels, surveys, a computerized "expert" system, job task/function analysis, and direct observation (pp. 99-104). A similar list of methodologies was articulated by van der Klink and Boon (2002) in their review of competency research and its use for the development of professional training curriculum. They mentioned conventional approaches such as Critical Incident interviewing, expert consultations, and the COMBI method, which focuses on both current core competencies required and on future competencies due to a rapidly changing context (pp. 414-415). If used appropriately, any of these methods will result in usable models.

The COMBI method raises an important point concerning the focus taken by the researcher engaged in competency research. Will the research focus on past behaviors that have resulted in high performance, and if so, how does one interpret those results in light of changing work environments?

Klemp illustrated the use of two approaches in the study of competency; supply side or a person-centered approach, and demand side or a context-centered approach. The supply side approach to competency describes the person who performs the work rather than the work that is being performed (Klemp, 2001 p. 132). This approach is very helpful in identifying the competencies that have allowed a particular individual to attain a high level of performance in a given context. The weakness is that the focus is on the past behavior of the individual does little to aid in developing a model that may address impending changes or challenges. The demand side approach, with its focus on the process by which tasks are performed, yields a better description of core skills, not only for the present, but also for the future (p. 137). This small shift in focus can make a significant difference in the research results and should be given careful attention as competency research is undertaken.

Established Competency Models

The referenced research methods have resulted in the establishment of a variety of models and lists of competencies that have been used in different ways. This review will briefly outline three of the most well-known general competency inventories and then look at a small representative sample of competency studies conducted for very specific contexts.

One of the first studies to produce a model for managerial competence was carried out by Boyatzis. The stated purpose was to "determine which characteristics of managers are related to effective performance in a variety of management jobs in a variety of organizations" (Boyatzis, 1983, p. 8). Boyatzis sought to identify the qualitative distinctives between poor, average, and high performers in a manner that would allow a better understanding of the competencies that separated high performers from average or poor performers. The end result was a text that outlined the theory of competence and job performance as it was understood at that point and provided a model that grouped competencies into six clusters. These were the goal and action management cluster, leadership cluster, human resources management cluster, directing subordinates cluster, focus on others cluster, and specialized knowledge cluster (p. 230).

Boyatzis' 1983 research focused on the role of the manager. This intentional focus was driven by Boyatzis' belief that the role of the manager would be particularly important in the emerging service economy (Boyatzis, 1983, p. 1). Boyatzis' desire was to provide the tools that would allow individuals to create a model for management that would lead to the development of competent managers, which would in turn lead to effective organizations. Boyatzis asserted that competent management was needed for an organization to reach its stated objectives (p. 1). The models in the text were not, according to Boyatzis, to be taken as conclusive, but rather as preliminary examples in the ongoing development of competency models that would lead to greater organizational effectiveness (p. 9). The study included over 2000 managers in 41 different management jobs in 12 different organizations (p. 229).

Each of the clusters identified by Boyatzis contained a set of competencies that was measured for degree of intensity in a particular management role. The results were delineated by managerial level (entry, middle, executive), by sector (private vs. public), by performance group (poor, average, superior), and by function (marketing, manufacturing, finance). The result was a measurable dataset that could be used to create a competency model showing which of the competencies in the various clusters were most likely to be present in superior performers. The Boyatzis data and resulting models were not designed as a means to assess the potential success of an individual, but rather to provide the means by which a model of the necessary competencies for a given role could be articulated.

The competencies identified by Boyatzis (1983) were aligned under the clusters outlined in Table 1 (p. 230). Boyatzis noted in his results the presence of what he defined as "threshold competencies" that were generic in nature, essential to success, but not causally related to superior performance (Boyatzis, 1983, p. 23). Threshold competencies were evident in managers, but their presence did not correlate to superior performance of the manager. The work done by Boyatzis laid the foundation for future studies in which competency models were further developed.

Table 1: Summary of Competency Results from Boyatzis

Cluster	Competency	Threshold Competency
Goal and action management	Concern with impact Diagnostic use of concepts Efficiency orientation Proactivity	
Leadership	Conceptualization Self-confidence Use of oral presentations	Logical thought
Human resource management	Managing group process Use of socialized power	Accurate self-assessment Positive regard
Directing subordinates		Developing others Spontaneity Use of unilateral power
Focus on other	Perceptual objectivity Self-control Stamina and adaptability	
Specialized knowledge		Specialized knowledge

One of the next major studies that established a research-based competency model for mangers was carried out by Harold Schroder in 1989 while he was at the University of South Florida. Schroder's study, which was based on three other studies, one of which was Boyatzis', established a four-cluster model with eleven competencies, as shown in Table 2.

The model proposed by Schroder covered many of the same concepts covered by Boyzatis, with greater attention being given to how managers deal with the process of gathering, refining, and using information than is evident in the Boyatzis model (Schroder, 1989, p. 81). This difference was seen in the first cluster, which contained the Cognitive Competencies. The last

Table 2: Summary of Competency Results from Schroder

Cluster	Competency
The Cognitive Competencies	Information Search
	Concept Formation
	Conceptual Flexibility
The Motivating Competencies	Interpersonal Search
	Managing Interaction
	Developmental Orientation
The Directional Competencies	Self-confidence
	Presentation
	Impact
The Achieving Competencies	Proactive Orientation
	Achievement Orientation

three clusters put forth by Schroder, which included the Motivating, Directional, and Achieving clusters, had multiple similarities with the work of Boyatzis.

The model presented by Schroder in 1989 represents a move forward in the understanding of competency models for managers in a couple of ways. First, while the model presented by Boyatzis was broader in the competencies identified, the clusters in Schroder's model were more refined in their definition and content than those presented by Boyatzis. Second, Schroder addressed in greater depth the key competencies required for success in "third wave" work environments. These key competencies include Conceptual Flexibility, Interpersonal Search, Managing Interaction, and Development Orientation. The common thread was the necessity of moving from a hierarchical approach of management to a shifting of responsibility downward in the organization (Schroder, 1989, p. 116). Schroder's model more accurately predicted the competencies required of managers in an environment driven by knowledge rather than by the production of material goods. Drucker (1994) viewed this paradigm as the emerging "knowledge society" (p. 64), while others such as Toffler referred to this change as "third wave" change (Schroder, 1989, p. 12). Some have noted that change is now an inherent part of the environment and that the rate of change is continuing to accelerate (Colteryahn & Davis, 2004, p. 31). The changing environment, regardless of its label, will require an equally dynamic set of competencies.

The next major work produced on competency models was published by Spencer and Spencer (1993). The major contribution made by this study was the further analysis of the data collected using the BEI. This analysis resulted in the competencies themselves being scaled, lower to higher, on three dimensions: intensity or completeness of action, size of impact, and complexity (Spencer & Spencer, 1993, p. 21). Each of the 21 competencies identified was scaled in one or more of these three dimensions. The position of a given action in the scale was determined by an individual trained in the coding methodology. The result was a scaled modeled with indicators for each competency allowing the measurement along the three dimensions. This setup enabled the researchers to more precisely identify not only the competencies themselves, but also the relative strength of competency for various roles.

Spencer and Spencer (1993) identified 21 generic competencies from their evaluation of 286 competency models available (p. 20). The 21 competencies were grouped around six clusters as shown in Table 3.

Table 3: Summary of Competency Results from Spencer and Spencer

Cluster	Competency
Achievement & Action	Achievement Orientation
	Concern for order, quality and accuracy
	Initiative
	Information seeking
Helping and Human Services	Interpersonal understanding
	Customer orientation
Impact and Influence	Impact and influence
	Organizational awareness
	Relationship building
Managerial	Developing others
	Directiveness
	Teamwork and cooperation
	Team leadership
Cognitive	Analytical thinking
	Conceptual thinking
	Technical/professional/managerial expertise
Personal Effectiveness	Self-control
	Self-confidence
	Flexibility
	Organizational commitment
	Other personal characteristics & competencies (pp.25-88)

The competencies were then used to create generic job competency models for a variety of fields. The researchers incorporated competencies from the original models identified after recoding using the new set of generic behavioral indicators

(Spencer & Spencer, 1993, p. 160). The generic job competency models in a variety of fields were intended to be used to compare the different occupations more than specific roles (p. 159). The models are helpful as a starting point in determining what competencies, and in what measure, would likely be found for a particular role. This is the value provided by Spencer and Spencer's work for researchers and those developing competency models. They also provided a good explanation of the research methodology used and specific steps on how to develop a competency model for a specific context (p. 95).

These three models were reviewed because of the research methodology employed in each study. These studies also utilized and built upon previous research, and each study provided generic competency models that would allow researchers and practitioners to alike to gain valuable insight from their work. The findings from these and other studies, such as the study by the American Society for Training and Development (Davis, Naughton, & Rothwell, 2004), have been refined and applied in a variety of contexts, as described in the next section.

Application and Use of Competency Models

The competencies discovered and the models developed through various studies have been used in a variety of ways, sometimes with a great deal of care and other times carelessly. This section of the paper explores the ways in which competency models have been applied and used in a variety of contexts. The literature reviewed demonstrated differences in the use of competency models based on geographical locations as well as organizational type.

Le Deist and Winterton (2005) described two distinct approaches to the use of competency within management. The authors found that management strategists emphasized competencies that were unique and related to a specific firm, while those concerned with human resource development sought to develop competencies that were transferable and required for most jobs (p. 28). While both groups may begin with a similar definition of competency, the different approach in usage leads to a very different application of the competency model.

The first of these approaches to competency serves to support the drive for strategic competitiveness by articulating core competencies needed by individuals in a particular role in a specific context. Having competent individuals in your organization can certainly result in a competitive advantage. The desire for a higher level of organizational competitiveness can be the foundation upon which the drive for individual competency is developed. Concentrating on the core competencies of the organization is one means of acquiring and maintaining a competitive edge (Bergenhenegouwen, Horn, & Mooijman, 1996, p. 29).

Prahaland and Hamel (1990) define core competence for an organization as "the collective learning in an organization, especially how to coordinate diverse production skills and integrate multiple streams of technology" (p. 82). Their particular emphasis on organizational competence stands alongside but distinct from individual competence. It is, however, important to understand that the collective organizational competency to which they refer is a composite of the competencies of the individuals present within the organization, along with environmental and technological factors (Bergenhenegouwen, Horn, & Mooijman, 1996, p. 30). There may be synergy created by a particular grouping of individuals gathering around a specific goal or purpose, but an organization itself cannot be competent without the people who compose the organization.

This use of competency, beginning with the organizational competencies required or desired, leads to a prescriptive approach in leadership development. The content and form of the competencies required in any given role are created with a view of the organizational strategy, structure, and culture, which includes the given management philosophy (Bergenhenegouwen, Horn, & Mooijman, 1996, p. 30). The starting point is the understanding what is required for the particular role and then finding the individual who fits, rather than assessing the competencies of the individual and then finding a suitable role. Even though both approaches have merit, the first is more in keeping with the approach of a management strategist as noted by Le Deist and Winter (2005). It may be possible to develop the necessary competencies in a particular individual for a particular role, but this can be a time-consuming process. As one HR professional observed, "It is easier to hire a squirrel than to train someone to climb a tree."

The second approach or use of leadership competency identified by Le Deist and Winterton (2005) is employed by those concerned with human resource development on a broader scale than just for a particular organization. This approach seeks to develop competencies that are transferable to roles in a number of different organizations (p. 28). The philosophy underlying this approach is that a certain number of generic competencies could be used in a number of settings and should be developed. This approach manifests itself in vocational education and training. The driving factors that influence this trend are global, with a strong European influence. European initiatives such as the Personal Skills Card and the European Skills Accrediting System are outcomes of this approach (p. 28).

Clearly, the use of a competency model is by no means confined to North America. Other parts of the world have also engaged in researching and applying the model. However, some clarification is needed when considering the research and application of competencies in other countries. An overview of the current definition and understanding of competency from an international perspective was undertaken by Le Deist and Winterton in 2005. They, along with others, have noted that there is much confusion and debate regarding competence, rendering it nearly impossible to arrive at a definition that accommodates all the ways in which the term is used (Dubois & Rothwell, 2004, p. 18; Le Deist & Winterton, 2005, p. 29; Norris, 1991, Introduction, para 4). The absence of standard procedures and philosophical understanding contributes to the existing confusion. Le Deist and Winterton's comparison of the ways in which competency is viewed in various countries has contributed to a better understanding of competency models.

As of 2010, three distinct approaches to competency are in use in various countries. These include the Behavioral Approach (US), the Functional Approach (UK), and a Multi-dimensional and Holistic Approach (France, Germany, and Austria). These models were described as being the "dominant" approaches to competency and began relatively independent of one another. In a chronological sense, research in the field of competency was first developed in the US, followed by the UK, and finally was adopted in continental Europe (Le Deist & Winterton, 2005, p. 31).

The Behavioral Approach as described by Le Deist and Winterton (2005) began in the United States with the work of McClelland as an alternative to cognitive testing used to predict occupational success (p. 31). This approach to competency sought to identify the skills and dispositions, apart from intelligence as determined by standardized tests, that contributed to success in the workplace. The skills and dispositions identified included factors such as self-awareness, self-regulation, and social skills (p. 31). McClelland (1998) concluded that executives could indeed increase their level of performance if competency areas of weakness were addressed (p. 336). This suggests that, unlike intelligence or personality, competencies that are viewed as behavioral in nature can be developed over time (Le Deist & Winterton, 2005, p. 31). The research by McClelland did not comment on the permanence of the changes in executives. It is not known whether the behavioral changes observed were still apparent more than two years after the initial study.

In response to inadequate skill formation in a variety of tasks, a slightly different approach to the use of competency was observed in the United Kingdom (UK). The competence-based approach was introduced in the 1980s in vocational education and training (VET) throughout the UK. The intent was to establish a nationwide system of uniform work-based qualifications (Le Deist & Winterton, 2005, p. 33). A number of roles were evaluated in an effort to develop the elements of competence support by performance indicators and range indicators. This system of vocational standards or qualifications was based on the reality of the workplace (Mansfield, 1993, p. 21). A weakness of the system has been the lack of participation by many employers because identified competencies lack alignment with a specific role. Educational institutions raised concerns regarding the weak theoretical underpinning of the competencies identified (Le Deist & Winterton, p. 34). The emphasis in establishing the National Vocational Qualifications (NVQ) was on the functional competence and the "ability to demonstrate performance to the standards required of employment in a work context" (Knasel & Meed as cited in Le Deist & Winterton, 2005, p. 34). There was tension in the UK because of the assertion that the functional competency approach did not address things such as individual values, personal understandings, and character qualities that are inherent in the individual and contribute to how a person performs in a given situation (p. 35). One response to this perceived shortcoming of the strictly functional approach to competency was the development of more holistic models. An example of the holistic model proposed includes the integration of knowledge, understanding, values, and skills that reside within the individual (Hodkinson & Issit, 1995, p. 149). The critique is that a functional approach does not sufficiently recognize inherent attributes of the individual and how these may impact a particular function.

Cheetham and Chivers (1996) attempted to bring together the outcomes approach to competencies that was prevalent in the NVQ and the reflective practitioner approach. This meant that both the functional and the behavioral perspectives on competency were included, along with demonstrating how meta-competence and ethics could be included in a holistic model of competence for professionals (p. 20). This amalgam was an attempt to synthesize what the authors perceived as seven main influences in the competency discussion. These influences included the UK occupational standards model, the job competence model, the behavioral model, the "reflective practitioner" approach, meta-competencies, core skills, and values or ethics at both a personal and professional level (p. 20). The resulting model attempted to show the relationship between four core components and their various elements or constituents with meta-competencies, which assist in the ongoing development of core competencies (p. 24).

The resulting holistic competency model was unique in that it attempted to show a potential relationship among meta-competencies, competencies, the outcomes or results of the competencies, and how reflection is an integral part of the process (see Figure 4). It was noted that the main purpose of reflection was to improve professional competence, which is closely aligned with outcomes (Cheetham & Chivers, 1996, p. 26). The significance of the work of Cheetham and Chivers was that it brought together several elements of the competency discussion into a model that served more than one profession by allowing the core components to flex (p. 27). The intent was to synthesize while allowing for flexibility.

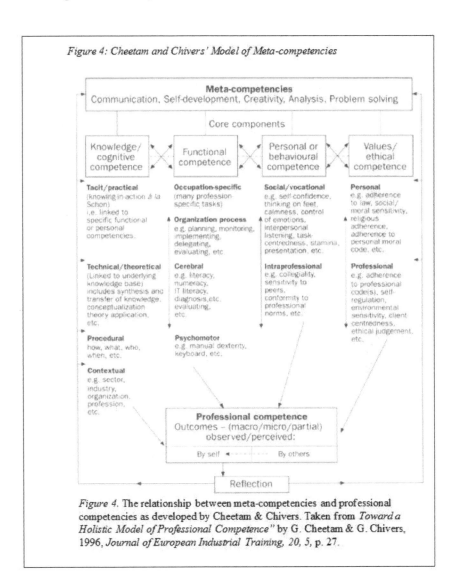

Figure 4: Cheetam and Chivers' Model of Meta-competencies

Figure 4. The relationship between meta-competencies and professional competencies as developed by Cheetam & Chivers. Taken from *Toward a Holistic Model of Professional Competence"* by G. Cheetam & G. Chivers, 1996, *Journal of European Industrial Training, 20,* 5, p. 27.

The American Society for Training and Development (ASTD) had commissioned its own study of the use and application of competency models, and published the results in the journal *T +D* (Davis, Naughton, & Rothwell, 2004). ASTD went on to advise that the competency model presented ought to guide the personal development of training professionals, as well as the development programs at an organizational level (Rothwell & Wellins, 2004, p. 4). The authors proposed that at the organizational level, competency models can serve to integrate all aspects of the HR process, right from earliest stages of role development to performance evaluation and promotion (p. 5). The authors also advocated for educators to base curriculum and other training programs on competency models developed with input from employers (p. 8). This aspect of application has been an essential element in European models (Boon and van der Klink, 2002; Le Deist & Winterton, 2005; Cheetham & Chivers, 1996; Cheetham & Chivers, 1998; Mansfield, 1993).

Competency models have become more useful in recent years because of the rapid and continuing changes in the work environment. New models of management have emerged that focus more on output and performance than on specific job assignments and tasks (Boon and van der Klink, 2002, p. 351). The flexibility required of the labor force can more easily be captured by using a competency frame than by relying on creating a specific list of tasks for each role within the organization. Adhering to very rigid job descriptions limits who can be hired and removes expectations at the individual level to adapt to the changing work environment. The flexibility that competency models allow in the hiring and training process is one factor cited by van der Klink and Boon as being responsible for the popularity of the concept (p. 353).

While the authors noted that respondents did cite competency models as being popular, at the same time the same respondents did not perceive them as being widely implemented. Barriers were identified as the high cost of implementation, along with the challenge of finding the appropriate time in the organizational business cycle to implement this approach to HR management (Boon and van der Klink, 2002, p. 353). Most often, when the money was available to make this type of reinvestment in the organization, things were functioning smoothly and the felt need for change was low. It is during the challenging times that the need for a different approach to management becomes apparent, but unfortunately these are also the times when there are fewer resources available to implement a competency model in the organization. The sector in which competency models are least applied is the nonprofit sector, for the reasons just noted (p. 353).

The field of education was another area of application of competency noted by Boon and van der Klink. The authors observed that respondents stated that competency models that originated in or had significant input from labor groups had a secondary benefit of establishing helpful dialogue and a common vocabulary. The respondents in this particular study viewed the adoption of competency models by educational institutions as a "communication tool" between business and education (Boon and van der Klink, 2002, p. 354). Adoption of the competency approach in education was also viewed as a means of addressing both the heavy emphasis on theoretical knowledge in the curriculum and the lack of practical training. It was felt that the application of a competency model would allow for this perceived imbalance to be addressed. Finding the appropriate balance of the theoretical and practical will continue to be an area of challenge for educators because the balance of these two important elements looks different in each field. It was also noted that while there would be benefits to using competency models when developing curriculum, there are few examples of that actually occurring (p. 354).

The benefits of allowing competency models to influence and shape educational process and outcomes have been noted, but challenges have been identified as well. Challenges include the lack of clarity regarding the concept of competency itself, obtaining a realistic set of competencies based on actual job demands, reaching the appropriate curricular balance between giving students information for their immediate professional needs and the skills needed for long-term professional growth, and keeping the competency profiles updated along with the corresponding curriculum (van der Klink & Boon, 2002, pp. 412-414). These challenges ought not to prohibit asking whether the demands of the marketplace align with the curriculum. In one exploration of this important relationship, the researchers discovered that graduates from a business program made little use of the statistical training in the curriculum (p. 421). This is an example of finding the appropriate balance between market demands and curricular breadth and depth that provides foundational knowledge not easily tied directly to job performance.

This section has explored some of the more general ways in which competency models have been viewed and applied to a variety of settings. There are a number of ways in which competency models have been used with positive results. The literature has also highlighted a number of challenges in the development and implementation of competency models in different settings. The appropriate and effective use of competency models, regardless of the setting, requires hard work and attention to both the strengths and the potential shortcomings of competency modeling. The next section highlights studies that have developed or applied competency models in reference to very specific roles. These are examples of applying competency models not in a general manner, but to specific roles and contexts.

Competency Studies for Specific Occupations or Roles

The literature regarding leadership competency contains examples of studies designed to measure the competencies required for a given task or situation. Competency models have been used as a means of predicting the success of construction project managers (Dainty, Cheng, & Moore, 2005). This UK study used a form of the BEI methodology to identify the competencies of project managers who displayed superior performance as determined by a panel of their colleagues (p. 4). The study identified 12 behaviors for construction project managers, with "self-control" and "team leadership" being the behaviors most predictive of success (p. 7). The study was viewed as a key component in moving the evaluation of success for project managers from being based strictly on cost, quality, and other quantitative measures, to one that with more robust measures of success centered on project completion measures that incorporate the competencies identified (p. 8). No longer would simply completing a project be viewed as the essence of success; how the project was completed would be considered as well.

Another study conducted in the United Kingdom concluded that there were discernable competencies related to current performance and other competencies tied to "promotability" among managers in three financial services companies (Robertson & Gibbons, 1999, p. 11). Understanding the distinction between competencies related to current performance and those for promotability allows practitioners to better evaluate current staff. A link between competencies and personality traits was also identified, showing that certain personality traits were more apparent in those having particular competencies (p. 12). The study found that those considered extroverts were more likely to be promoted than were those who were conscientious knowledge experts (p.12). Long-term use of this pattern in promotion and advancement in an organization can result in organizational weaknesses that will need to be addressed. The weakness created is a lack of expert knowledge at the highest levels of an organization. While such a lack is not necessarily fatal for an organization, the danger does need to be identified as a means of compensating for this tendency implemented. Diligent use of a well-developed competency model could be one solution.

A study of additional example of an application of competency models to a specific occupation was conducted by Holmes (2005). In this study, competencies for emerging practice in the field of occupational therapy were identified by current professionals in the field (p. 19). The result was an initial list of 104 competencies that were assigned to one of six categories. Through two more rounds of weighting and ranking, the competence of greatest importance was identified in each category (p. 204). This information was used to propose ideas for the refinement of training programs and the development of professional standards that would better prepare individuals for future challenges in the field of occupational therapy. This study also identified strategies that could be employed in the development of the identified competencies (p. 208).

In a study done to measure the effectiveness of training for nurses, the focus was on 12 competencies as the measure of job performance for nurses in a large, regional university medical center (Krejci & Malin, 1997, p. 237). The competencies were selected as a means of measuring the development of leadership capacity for nurses in two areas deemed by the researchers to be essential in the developing medical field. The two areas of focus were the development of systems thinking and the overcoming of oppressed group behaviors (p. 236). Since the purpose of the study was to measure the effectiveness of a training program, participants were surveyed before and after their training. A three-month follow-up was also done to assess the permanence of the changes observed (p. 239). This study illustrates competence measures as a means of establishing job performance standards for the purpose of measuring a factor other than personal performance.

While these studies were not intended to measure the specific competencies for a leader within a nonprofit organization, they have shown efforts to assess competencies in a systematic manner. These studies illustrate how mastery of various leadership competencies by leaders can be measured in a variety of sectors and professions.

Critique of the Competency Approach

It is not surprising that with so much being written about the competency approach, some misunderstandings and less than helpful interpretations of the role of competence should arise. How competence is viewed and used must be carefully understood. The absence of accurate definitions and understandings of competence can lead to misunderstandings and to wrong application of the competency theory to practice, resulting in a general mistrust of the whole concept of competence as a means of assessment for service in a variety of contexts. These misperceptions and the resulting criticisms must be examined with a view toward correcting wrong ideas, but also allowing the criticism to aid in the refining of competency theory and practice.

Many criticisms of the competency approach stem from misunderstandings and inaccurate perceptions. Kolligian and Sternberg (1990) noted that "over the past few decades some researchers have gone so far as to characterize the search for competence as *the* basic motivation for behavior" (p. ix). This is a very limited view of competence and ignores other factors, such as context and hard skills, relevant to a given role. While it is true that motivation was one of the elements in a classic definition of competence, it must be supplemented with other factors such as traits, self-concept, content knowledge, and behavioral skills (Spencer, McClelland, & Spencer, 1994, p. 6) in order to round out the competence approach. Competence must be viewed as more than just a search for the right behaviors. An appropriately nuanced definition of competence is critical to having a proper understanding and application of the competence to leadership.

Another source of criticisms is what some perceive as the subjective nature of competency theory and its application. Considerable discussion has taken place regarding the competence of teachers, students, workers, and leaders/managers. The concerns center on how to determine whether an individual exemplifies competence. The criticism is that the process of determining whether an individual is "competent" is too subjective and too dependent on the individual doing the assessment. In some respects it is understandable that those who do not understand the research base upon which competency theory and practice is based would arrive at this conclusion. The process leading to a label of "competent" or "incompetent" ought to employ a rigorous, validated process and should not simply be a matter of using a checklist. The process must take into account the complex interaction of tasks performance, the context in which they are performed, and all the interpersonal dynamics inherent in a given role (Sternberg, 1990, p. 117).

Sternberg (1990), who is a strong supporter of competence models, noted another danger of competency models that include some type of objective measure as the primary instrument. An example would be the use of a standard intelligence test. These types of measures can leave people who possess a good deal of competence that is measurable when subjective abilities are taken into consideration, feeling inferior or incompetent if only the objective portion of the evaluation is taken into consideration (p. 137). The use of competence prototypes based solely on intelligence tests, while useful in an academic setting, may not be particularly useful outside the school environment (p. 145). This point echoes one of chief concerns articulated by McClelland (1973) when he first proposed competency testing as a means of measuring or predicting job performance.

Competency also has elements of perception and context that need to be considered. The behavior viewed as evidence of competence in one culture may not be viewed the same way in another culture or context (Sternberg, 1990, p. 144; Raven, 2001a, p. 167). The subjective nature of competency models can be a great strength in that individuals have opportunity to demonstrate competency in ways other than through objective, standardized tests. Ensuring that competency models take into consideration the factors beyond mere content knowledge is the key in establishing a credible competency measure. The matters of context and perception lead to difficulty when a person tries to transfer a competency model from one context to another without giving careful consideration to what adjustments are required for the model to be a valid measure of competence in the new context.

Another area of criticism leveled at the use of competency models revolves around implementation. One danger of competency models is that much time and effort are spent on developing models that are never implemented (Zemke & Zemke, 1999, p. 76). Zemke and Zemke noted, "Indeed, if you have done any reading or research on this subject, it may strike you that far more attention is paid to the issue of developing competency models than to the issue of using them" (p. 71). Developing credible competency models is expensive, hard work; to fail to use the model is to waste the learning that has taken place, along with the time and money invested. This, however, is exactly what happens, and the result is that the competency model approach as an HR strategy is viewed as yet another fad in the business world. In many ways, this critique of competency models is justified. Implementing competency models requires a great deal of work, and when an organization does not complete the process, the result is more damage than benefit.

The critique of competency models as a method of identifying top performers has been aimed at the very foundation of the movement. Barrett and Depinet (1991) took issue with key aspects of McClelland's argument for competency measures as opposed to intelligence tests being the best indicators of job performance (McClelland, 1973). Barrett and Depinet identified five "themes" from McClelland and proceed to offer evidence that McClelland was wrong in his assertions. The five themes suggested that (a) grades in school did not predict occupational success, (b) intelligence tests and aptitude tests did not predict occupational success or other important life outcomes, (c) test and academic performance only predicted job performance as a result of an underlying relationship to social status, (d) traditional tests are unfair to minorities, and (e) "competencies" would more successfully predict important behaviors than would more traditional tests (Barrett & Depinet, 1991, p. 1012).

In their critique, Barrett and Depinet used a variety of studies to point out what they viewed to be fundamental weaknesses in foundational elements of McClelland's case for competency measures. They noted that McClelland neglected to consider key studies (Barrett & Depinet, 1991, p. 1012), overlooked key points in a referenced study (p. 1014), and did not adequately define competency in this initial piece (p. 1019). The conclusion of Barrett and Depinet was that McClelland "must present empirical data to support his conclusions" (p. 1021).

McClelland would later respond to the challenge of Barrett and Depinet, but in a more general way. McClelland first pointed out that the intent of his publication was not to present a finished model, but to argue that competency-based assessment should be developed as an alternative to "academic-type testing" (McClelland, 1998, p. 331). McClelland further demonstrated how competency assessment as undertaken using the Behavioral Event Interview (BEI) can be used to provide a competency model that can predict the success of an individual in a role for which a competency model has been developed. The study that McClelland used showed how the use of a competency model helped to reduce executive turnover from 49% to just over 6% when it was implemented in the hiring process (p. 336). While McClelland did build a case that showed the validity of the competency model approach in a particular setting, the limitations of the outlined model were noted as well (p. 338). It cannot be assumed that a competency model developed for use in a particular setting is readily transferable without considerable adjustments. This study will clarify some of those necessary adjustments in perspective that might need to be made for those working in the nonprofit sector.

Ree and Earles (1992) made a case that challenged McClelland's perspective on the validity of intelligence tests as the best measure of job performance. The authors made a distinction between possessing the skills, knowledge, and techniques needed for job performance apart from the actual performance or application of the skills in a particular work role (p. 87). In their rebuttal, Stenberg and Wagner (1993) noted that Ree and Earles are not alone in their assertion that the use of intelligence tests alone will lead to maximized job performance (p. 1). Ree and Earles clearly indicated that intelligence testing is most effective for predicting the effectiveness of training success, but less so for predicting job accomplishment or task accomplishment. While they noted a moderate statistical correlation (.33) between intelligence testing and job or task accomplishment, this correlation was much less than the correlation for measuring job training success, which was .76 (Ree & Earles, 1992, p. 88).

In his original article, McClelland (1973) asserted that intelligence tests that can measure academic ability do not necessarily measure job performance (p. 4). The arguments put forth by Ree and Earles (1992) are challenged on the grounds that intelligence tests measure what an individual knows, but not necessarily what he or she can do. Intelligence tests can measure only a portion of what is needed to evaluate job effectiveness or performance. There are so many other factors that contribute to job success. Asserting that intelligence is the best or the main factor ignores many other elements. This is the main course of argument made in rebuttal to Ree and Earles (McClelland, 1993; Sternberg & Wagner, 1993).

Competency models and their use in organizations have been critiqued for other reasons as well. Cockerill, Hunt, and Schroder (1995) take issue with the lack of clarity regarding the type of managerial competency being assessed and the process by which competency models are developed. The authors observed that current competency models are actually measuring two types of competencies, but little is done to distinguish between types that contribute to confusion during implementation. Cockerill et al. noted that a distinction needs to be made between what they termed "threshold" and "high performance" competencies. Threshold competency is defined as "a cluster of related behavior which is used by the job holder but has not been found empirically to be associated with superior job performance" (p. 2). High performance competencies are those clustered behaviors that have been empirically proven to be present in high performing job holders, and absent or less developed in average performers (p. 2).

This critique is fair and helpful. Too often competency models are identified and put in place without sufficient thought regarding the application of the models. Threshold competencies are useful for hiring entry-level individuals, with no concern for whether the particular competencies being noted will lead to anything other than average or acceptable job performance. On the other hand, a competency model falling into the high performance category would be able to identify the behaviors, skills, abilities, and attitudes necessary not just for adequate performance, but for superior performance. This model would need to be empirically supported to justify the title of a high performance competency. The connection of the competencies to evaluated job performance is the key difference. For the high performance competency model to be developed, some level of criterion evaluation as noted by McClelland (1973) is necessary, which will entail more effort and expense (pp. 7-8).

Cockerill et al. (1995) offered a further appraisal of the use of competency models by placing the researchers and practitioners into one of three groups: Traditionalists, Inventors, and Scientists (p. 2). The authors are advocates of competency models for recruitment, development, and promotion but do take issue with how competency models are developed by two of the three groups mentioned. The main critique leveled is the lack of scientific rigor and empirical research incorporated into the development process of models by some who advocate for competency. The author's grouping of practitioners noted above revealed in broad strokes the various methodologies employed.

Traditionalists are viewed by Cockerill et al. (1995) as those who base the competencies on the actions of those who have progressed upward in the organization rapidly, with little or no regard for actual job performance. The criteria for inclusion within this model had more to do with upward promotion of individuals than with the measured success of job responsibilities. Cockerill et al. viewed the Traditionalist approach as inadequate because the criteria of job advancement as the test of a "competent" manager gives an inordinate amount of attention to behaviors related to self-promotion rather than to the behaviors needed to raise the performance of the unit and organization substantially (p. 4). This approach to competency results in the placement of a manager who may advance well through the organizational ranks, but does not necessarily contribute to the accomplishment of organizational goals, which ought to be a primary measure of success.

Inventors were characterized as those whose main desire was to introduce a new approach to hiring and advancement into an organization. Inventors fixate so much on bringing in the new they display little concern for having competencies were "empirically defensible" (Cockerill et al., 1995, p. 2). The lack of empirical methodology plagues this type of practitioner as well. The authors also stated that 95% of competencies used today have not followed a basic methodology that would lead to validated competencies (p. 9). The inadequacy of the model developed by inventors is embedded in the very development process often employed. The authors noted that Inventors seek to first predict the state of the organization 5-10 years into the future and then determine the competencies needed to lead in that environment (p. 6). The flaw in this approach is the lack of certainty regarding the actual organizational environment that far into the future. Even if an accurate prediction were made, an organization would need a manager with the skills to navigate the change required between the present and the future reality.

Cockerill et al. (1995) contended that eleven high performance managerial competencies (HPMC) exist that are applicable in any organization, industry, or country (p. 4). These competencies do not focus on the content or activities of the manger's role but rather on the competencies required to manage change, which is why they are broadly applicable. The shortcoming of competency models that Cockerill et al. sought to address is the lack of scientific rigor in the development of models. The authors suggest as a starting point their eleven managerial competencies as a valid means by which to measure job performance. They also advocate for a more rigorous approach based on organizational success in the development of competency models (p. 11). It is the Scientist group that would make use of the validated competency models such as the ones offered by Cockerill et al.

While this advice should be heeded, it is worth noting that while the eleven HPMC's advocated by Cockerill et al. have been validated, there could be additional competencies that would provide additional clarity for a particular role — providing the appropriate steps are taken in the development process. Cockerill et al. see great opportunity for the implementation and use of competencies models, but have called for careful, thoughtful, and rigorous process in the development of the models. What seems to be missing from their work is any serious discussion as to how the "person" of the leader fits into competency models.

Raven (2001a) noted a number of implications of the competency studies completed to date. These include a preoccupation with "low level" competencies that focus too narrowly on a given role while ignoring the broader context (p. 168) and a realistic understanding of the limitations of research methodologies in current use (p. 166). Raven recognized the value of competencies, but at the same time raised concerns that a focus on the competency list alone can result in reductionist thinking (p. 167).

Tribe (2001) articulated other concerns regarding the use of the competency- based approach in the training of lawyers. The main shortcoming in the manner in which lawyers were trained, in Tribe's opinion, was the lack of assessment focusing on the desired competencies. The underlying cause was the absence of objective criteria by which to measure the degree to which a law student possessed a given competence (p. 156). Rather than rising to the challenge of carefully and clearly breaking down a desired competency into the individual skills and the behaviors required of each, along with a means of measuring each item, there was a reversion to low level, easy-to-measure items that do not address the challenges of practicing one's profession in a broader, dynamic context (Raven, 2001a, p. 166). The work involved in developing such a systematic and dynamic approach to professional training is daunting and therefore is rarely undertaken.

All competency inquiry must rest on a foundation of solid methodology that has been determined to return accurate and valid results. No methodology can be viewed as perfect, and when shortcomings in methodology are discovered, these must be acknowledged and accounted for. Raven (2001a) briefly highlighted an often-overlooked weakness of Critical Incident Interviewing (CII) and Behavioral Event Interviewing (BEI). These methods have been established as credible means of identifying the competencies evident in the highest performers, in contrast with those who are not. What these methods fail to uncover is the contribution made to the success of the high performers by those around them who would not be considered high performers (p. 166). The contributions of others do have an impact on the observable performance of team members. The interplay between individuals in a given context is difficult to measure, and therefore it is difficult to assess how this might influence the competencies identified for a given individual. Not only do individuals in a given context make a contribution to one another's success, but they also contribute to the transformation of one another and of the context (p. 166). These limitations of CII and BEI must not be ignored by the researcher.

This review of literature critical of competency models served to show that while competency models have much to offer, weaknesses have been identified in the development and application of competency models. The challenges to the foundational notions upon which competency testing was built must be answered thoughtfully and with credible evidence. Critiques such as these must be taken seriously, evaluated, and then clearly answered. Free and open debate has served to strengthen the competency model movement, as is the case with all ideas that are allowed to be discussed with the aspiration of strengthening theory and practice.

Summary

The literature review provided the information necessary for a more thorough understanding of key elements in this study. The background and history of the nonprofit sector were developed in this review. The nonprofit sector has been described as one of three sectors present in modern society and has been operating alongside the public and private sector for many years. However, in the last 50 years, the nonprofit sector has experienced significant growth. The nonprofit sector as a whole is now a major employer in the United States, and as such is receiving far more attention than before. With the attention has come a greater emphasis on accountability and attention to mission. This increased attention to outcomes has created an environment of rapid change for most nonprofits in the areas of planning, accounting, public relations, and effective delivery of services. The skill set needed by nonprofit executives is beginning to resemble more closely the roles of their counterparts in business and government. The research and literature dedicated to understanding the role of nonprofit leaders has not kept pace with the growth in the sector, resulting in a patchwork approach to leadership development in the nonprofit sector as a whole. Addressing this shortfall is imperative if the leadership needs of the nonprofit sector are to be met in the coming years by people who are adequately prepared to lead in a challenging and changing environment.

The literature review also explored what a variety of authors have written regarding the role of nonprofit leaders. Debate continues regarding whether leading in a nonprofit is substantially different from leading in other sectors. What is not debated is the lack of research in the area of nonprofit leadership and its unique challenges. Some authors such as Nanus and Dobbs (1999) have presented a model, but as of mid-2010 this model has not been tested. Other theories of leadership, such as servant-leadership, have something to offer as well; but again, there has been no research aimed specifically at the nonprofit leaders to investigate the fit of these models with actual roles in the nonprofit. The future growth and health of the sector necessitate developing a model that will give a more comprehensive picture of the motives, traits, self-concept, knowledge, and skills necessary to lead.

The historical development of the notion of competency was covered in the review. The literature demonstrated how the idea that predicting performance based on something more than intelligence tests has resulted in the competency models' being used primarily in business and government. The increasing complexity of competency models has restricted the use of models to sectors with the available resources to fund the development of helpful models. Many leadership models developed have been labeled as competency models, but they lack many of the distinguishing characteristics of a true competency model. This is due in part to lack of resources, but also to a lack of understanding regarding the true nature of competency models. Creating well-developed competency models for use in an organization requires a good deal of time, money and expertise. Poorly developed models lead to disappointing results, tarnishing the reputation of competency models as a proven mechanism for leadership recruitment and development. This study endeavors to contribute a valid competency model for nonprofit leaders. Chapter three develops the methodology for this study.

Chapter Three

Methodology

The purpose of this study was to establish a competency model for executive leaders within the social service segment of the nonprofit sector. The social service sector provides care and services for those in greatest need in society. The services provided include, but are not limited to, daycare, personal counseling, job training, child protection, programming for children, and rehabilitation (Smith, 2002, p. 153). Input and feedback from those currently or recently in leadership positions was used to identify, from a practitioners' perspective, the competencies required for effective leadership within the nonprofit sector. Using this information, a competency model was developed to foster the recognition and development of the identified competencies for nonprofit leaders.

The research questions that flowed from the purpose of this study were:

Research question #1: What competencies are needed for executives to lead effectively in the social service organization in the nonprofit sector?

Research question #2: How do the competencies as identified by leaders in a particular nonprofit sector compare with competency lists formulated for similar roles in other sectors?

Research question #3: Can a set of competencies unique to nonprofit organizations be identified for use in recruitment and development of nonprofit leaders?

Research Methods

The Delphi method has been noted as being most useful in dealing with problems or issues that are ill-defined or have little knowledge on which to base a decision or plan of action (Ziglio, 1996, p. 3). This conclusion renders a positivist approach to this particular set of research questions untenable because of the absence of existing research related to competencies for nonprofit, executive leaders. The philosophical frame undergirding this study was a constructivist approach. The constructivist approach falls into the post-positivist paradigm and holds that views of the world are constructed based on experiences and interactions (Trochim, 2006). The Delphi method allows for the construction and refinement of ideas or an understanding of a given phenomenon utilizing the experience of experts. By garnering and refining the ideas of experts concerning a given topic, new knowledge and understanding can be developed that can guide future action. Thus the Delphi method relies heavily on the constructivist foundation.

Babbie (2004) outlined three primary purposes of social research: exploration, description, and explanation (p. 87). It is possible for a study to accomplish more than one of these functions because the differences between these purposes are not always readily apparent. This study fell largely into the exploration and description categories. The preliminary survey gathered descriptive information that helped to shape and form the more exploratory portion of the study, which used the Delphi method.

The study included two distinct phases of data collection. In the first phase of the study, data was gathered from a wide range of individuals associated with the nonprofit social sector. The intention was not only to gather an overview of the sector from the perspective of practitioners in the field, but also to recruit a panel of qualified individuals to serve on the expert panel. This panel consisted of experts for the next phase of the study utilizing the Delphi method, which sought to define the competencies for nonprofit social services sector executive-level leaders.

The Preliminary Survey

A preliminary survey was used in the study to allow the collection of more general data pertaining to social sector nonprofit organizations in the Pacific Northwest. It functioned as a recruitment and screening tool for the creation of the expert panel required for the Delphi portion of the study.

Survey research has been characterized as being the best method to collect original data describing a population that cannot be directly observed (Babbie, 2004, p. 243). Although this particular methodology has strengths that make it attractive, it also has inherent weaknesses. Surveys do not always take into consideration the social context of the respondent, so in this regard they can be inflexible (Babbie, 2004, p. 275) Babbie also notes that surveys are generally weak on validity, but strong on reliability (p. 275). This particular weakness can be minimized by the type of information requested. A survey can have a higher validity if the information requested is fact-based such as the number of times the participant has engaged in a particular activity, as opposed to his or her opinion rated on a Likert scale. People's opinions do not always fall within the parameters established in the survey, making the measurement artificial (p. 275). This limitation has been noted in other research projects as well (Abbott, 2009, p. 299; Skogen & Thrane, 2008, pp. 16-17).

The researcher must also acknowledge that the results can be generalized only to the population that was surveyed. To generalize beyond this population represented by the sample is not a credible use of the results of the study (Creswell, 1994, p. 117). The researcher must consider the use of the results early in the design phase to ensure that an appropriate population and sample are chosen. A well-chosen survey sample using a standardized questionnaire can enable the researcher to make assertions about a particular group, such as a city, a particular subgroup, or even a national grouping (Babbie, 2004, p. 274). The end use or the application of the survey results needs to be considered in the design phase to ensure the necessary outcomes.

The usefulness of the survey outcomes was also affected by the response rates. A poor response rate jeopardizes the usefulness of the survey by bringing into question whether the returned survey truly represent the population being studied (Babbie, 2004, p. 261). The literature contains no universally set survey response rate though Babbie suggests that in general a 50 percent rate is acceptable. An acceptable rate of return for a particular study must be set by the researcher in consultation with the literature.

The validity and reliability of a study are built not only on the sample selection process and response rate, which have already been discussed, but also on the level of artificiality of the survey. Babbie (2004) noted that artificiality has two aspects: First, not all topics are best researched using a survey methodology; and second, the very act of asking questions regarding a given topic can influence the results (p. 275). The researcher must minimize or at least acknowledge these aspects of artificiality in the overall survey process.

The Delphi Method

The second phase of the study used the Delphi method. This approach is particularly useful in areas in which there was little or no commonly held knowledge on a given topic. Linstone and Turoff (2002a) explained, "Delphi may be characterized as a method for structuring a group communication process so that the process is effective in allowing a group of individuals, as a whole, to deal with a complex problem" (p. 3). This process allows the establishment of a base of information from which further research may be done, or an understanding about a challenging problem may emerge. The key to effective implementation of the Delphi method is the use of expert panels to gather information and opinions on a given topic with the goal of arriving at a consensus regarding the research question (Adler & Ziglio, 1996; Holmes, 2005; Linstone & Turoff, 2002b; Novakowski & Wellar,

2008; Williams & Webb, 1994). The selection of participants will be discussed later in the chapter.

Background of the Delphi Method

The origin of the Delphi methodology has been traced by a number of researchers to the RAND Corporation in the 1950s as a means of forecasting or predicting through the use of experts in a particular field (Critcher & Gladstone, 1998, p. 432; Linstone & Turoff, 2002a, p. 10; Novakowski & Wellar, 2008, p. 1485; Williams & Webb, 1994, p. 181). This methodology was developed for use in areas in which there was no established data or common foundational knowledge that allowed for predictive modeling. Dalkey and Helmer (1963) published a paper that showed the development of defensive strategy during the Cold War. The military did not have any type of relevant experience in dealing with the strategy issues because the world had never seen a situation that evolved into the Cold War following the close of World War II. One of the first papers outlined the technique as it had been used at the RAND Corporation in the development of defense strategy during the Cold War period. The Delphi method was an ideal means of gathering the input of experts and refining it to a point of consensus.

Linstone and Turoff (2002a) enumerated the reasons or circumstances that could make the Delphi method a good choice in dealing with a particular issue. These included:

> a) The problem does not lend itself to precise analytical techniques but cart [*sic*] benefit from subjective judgments on a collective basis

b) The individuals needed to contribute to the examination of a broad or complex problem have no history of adequate communication and may represent diverse backgrounds with respect to experience or expertise

c) More individuals are needed than can effectively interact in a face-to-face exchange

d) Time and cost make frequent group meetings infeasible

e) The efficiency of face-to-face meetings can be increased by supplemental group communication process

f) Disagreements among individuals are so severe or politically unpalatable that the communication process must be refereed and/or anonymity assured

g) The heterogeneity of the participants must be preserved to assure validity of the results, i.e., avoidance of domination by quantity or by strength of personality ("bandwagon effect") (p. 4).

Ziglio (1996) noted the Delphi method's usefulness for problems that have "no monitored history nor adequate information" that would guide current understanding or future practice (p. 4). It can be surmised, then, that the Delphi method is very useful for topics that have not yet been adequately studied to have evoked a defining body of literature. This absence may be due to the rapidly changing nature of the topic, or to its truly being an emerging field.

The literature outlines a variety of strengths associated with the Delphi method. These include the encouragements of open and honest feedback free from peer pressure (Williams &

Webb, 1994, p. 181). The method also can minimize strong emotions or unhelpful interpersonal dynamics within the panel. Not only does Delphi lend itself to problems that lack a well-developed knowledge base, but it also aids in overcoming issues related to a geographically dispersed expert panel and allows the researcher to bring together experts from diverse backgrounds who can contribute to the discussion group (Critcher & Gladstone, 1998, p. 432; Linstone & Turoff, 2002a, p. 4; Powell, 2003, p. 377; Ziglio, 1996, p. 22).

The fact that Delphi does not require meetings of the participants and that all responses reviewed by the group are kept anonymous can allow for a diversity of opinions to be fairly and carefully considered on the basis of their own merits. This was viewed as a strength of Delphi by Dalkey (1968) when he noted that face-to-face discussions have "serious drawbacks" (p. 3). The drawbacks cited were the influence of dominant individuals, noise, and group pressure toward conformity (p. 3). Dalkey viewed the development of the Delphi method as a means of reducing the negative aspects of face-to-face discussions while still being able to benefit from the collective group wisdom on a given subject. The three key features of Delphi that Dalkey put forth were the anonymity of responses, the controlled feedback of all group responses back to the group for further reflection and input over several rounds, and the statistical expression of the group opinion (p. 4). The Delphi method also allows panel members to retract, alter, or add to earlier comments after further reflection (Gibson & Miller, 1990, p. 35; Williams & Webb, 1994, p. 181).

The Delphi method stands in contrast to a focus group on two significant points. First, focus groups are typically done face-to-face, which means that group dynamics can play a role in the results. Second, focus groups most often are used to gain feedback from a group of qualified individuals on a particular message, topic, or product that is already developed (Edmunds, 1999, p. 2). The focus group gives feedback on what is presented to its members. They are not expected to create or refine, though their feedback may be used by others to do just that. For this particular set of research questions, the Delphi method was a good methodological fit.

Delphi Research Process

Two forms of the Delphi method have been used. The first is the conventional Delphi. The second is a more recent form called the conference Delphi, which utilizes some type of technology to compile and share responses with participants without the need to develop a questionnaire for each new round. Regardless of the form used, there are four distinct phases in the process. Linstone and Turoff (2002a) outlined the phases in the following manner:

> The first phase is characterized by exploration of the subject under discussion, wherein each individual contributes additional information he or she feels is pertinent to the issue. The second phase involves the process of reaching an understanding of how the groups views the issue (i.e., where the members agree or disagree and what they mean by relative terms such as importance,

desirability, or feasibility). if [*sic*] there is significant disagreement, then that disagreement is explored in the third phase to bring out the underlying reasons for the differences and possibly to evaluate them. The last phase, a final evaluation, occurs when all previously gathered information has been initially analyzed and the evaluations have been fed back for consideration. (pp. 5-6)

Novakowski and Wellar (2008) outlined three types of Delphi exercises that could be implemented as either conventional or conference Delphi. The broad categories include:

a) Normative Delphi—The exercise explores what should be. The goal is to obtain consensus about a preferred future state or process.

b) Forecasting Delphi—This form of the exercise is concerned with predictions about future events. Typically there is little very little, diverse or conflicting knowledge on the given topic. The original Delphi research projects concerning Soviet bombing strategies are a good example of this category (Dalkey & Helmer, 1963, p. 458).

c) Policy Delphi—This evaluates matters of political interest or consequence. The purpose is not necessarily consensus but rather to ensure that the full range of variables, opinions, and contexts of a particular issue are explored. (Novakowski & Wellar, 2008, p. 1486)

Though each of these exercises has a slightly different focus, the basic overall structure of the process remains. They all include group communication, anonymity of the participants, iteration, and movement of the group toward a central tendency (Novakowski & Wellar, 2008, p. 1487). Certain accommodations or alterations may be made in the specific methodology for each based on the context, but the overall structure ought to remain intact. This study fit into the Normative Delphi category.

A review of several studies that have utilized the Delphi method revealed a variety of approaches to methodology. It has been noted that there is no standard Delphi method in place that a researcher is expected to follow (Hasson, Keeney, & McKenna, 2000, p. 1009; Keeney, Hasson, & McKenna, 2006. p. 208; Powell, 2003, p. 377). The variations in methodology include the number of rounds, the size of the expert panels used, the types of questions asked, and the amount of structure incorporated in each round. There are, however, four steps that are common to any Delphi but may take on very different forms depending on the desired outcome. The steps include designing the questionnaire, identifying the participants, monitoring the participation, and tabulating the responses (Olshfski & Joseph, 1991, p. 298).

Reliability and Validity of Delphi

The Delphi method has not been without its critics. Proponents of the Delphi method realized that those who had a very traditional view of scientific method would struggle with the Delphi method (Linstone, 2002). The best known critique of the Delphi was made by Sackman (1975). He charged that the method was guilty of not following scientific method (Ziglio, 1996, p. 13) and of not having a universal, stable methodology (Goodman, 1987, p. 731). The scientific method, which is viewed as stable and universal, is characterized by a process or method of inquiry in which only measureable, observable data are considered as valid in the research enterprise (Babbie, 2004, p. 6; Trochim, 2006). Goodman also expands on Sackman's critique of the expert panels used in Delphi. The issues raised concerning the panels included the arbitrary nature of how an expert is defined, that anonymity can lead to a lack of accountability, and the potential that panel members could intentionally manipulate the results by giving extreme responses that would move the median results (pp. 732-733). The subject of the qualities of an "expert" as it pertains to this study will be developed later in the chapter.

The critique by Sackman (1975) was answered by Goldschmidt (1975), who chided Sackman with the comment, "He does what he criticizes Delphi practitioners for doing in their work" (p. 196). Goldschmidt pointed out that Sackman was using a journalistic approach, taking quotations out of context, using incorrect inferences, and making use of findings that were not properly cited to build his case against the Delphi method. Goldschmidt rebutted Sackman by addressing each of the ten questions Sackman raised and demonstrating shortcomings in his arguments against the Delphi method. While Goldschmidt did not see Sackman's work as being a sound critique of the Delphi method, he did acknowledge that if the practitioners of the Delphi method became more aware of and judicious in their methods, benefit from the critique would have been realized (Goldschmidt, 1975, p. 212).

One of the issues raised regarding Delphi concerns the level of reliability that is attainable with the method. Some researchers claim that there is no evidence of the reliability of the Delphi method (Hasson, Keeney, & McKenna, 2000, p. 1012; Williams & Webb, 1994, p. 182), meaning that if the same information were given to another panel, the results might or might not be the same; there is no way of knowing what the outcome would be. The lack of confidence in the reliability of the Delphi method may be attributed in part to the lack of recent studies on the theoretical and methodological aspects of Delphi (Ziglio, 1996, p. 16). Ziglio indicated that it has been assumed that group judgments are more reliable than individual judgments (p. 15). It has also been suggested that application of certain criteria used in qualitative studies could help ensure that credible results are produced (Hasson, Keeney, & McKenna, 2000, p. 1013).

Gibson and Miller (1990) reported that the objective validity of a Delphi study would be very difficult to assess. Though the results may not be able to be examined quantitatively, it should be remembered that Delphi is best used for problems that suffer from a scarcity of data (p. 41). The authors went on to suggest that possible criteria for success would be the "usefulness" of the data and the satisfaction of the participants with the process and the results of the process. This argument relies heavily on the assumption that in the absence of any definitive information on a given topic, what has been learned through a Delphi study would be helpful in providing direction.

The Delphi method can be methodologically rigorous; when this approach is taken, concerns regarding the outcomes can be minimized. Different researchers have highlighted different methodological steps that must be followed carefully to ensure valid results. Goodman (1987) cited the selection of the panel, the way in which the panel's responses were compiled, and how consensus was built; Powell (2003) highlighted having a robust research procedure, careful selection of the expert panel, and careful data analysis procedures; and Ziglio (1996) pointed to the selection of the panel, reliability of outcomes, and instructions given to the experts on the panel.

One of the areas in which the Delphi method exhibits flexibility is the size of the expert panel deemed appropriate. The size of the expert panels have varied greatly in studies that have been done; one study was reported to have had 1,985 participants (Williams & Webb, 1994, p. 181), while others had as few as 5. The typical Delphi study falls in the 10-30 range, with some studies using fewer than 10 participants (Hansen & Reynolds, 2010; Hayes, 2007; Gibson & Miller, 1990; Olshfski & Joseph, 1991; Williams & Webb, 1994). Ziglio (1996) contended that good results can be attained with a panel of 10-15 experts. He did also express that a larger panel resulted in less error, but at some point the addition of more members provided marginal benefit (p. 14). Novakowski and Wellar (2008) asserted that the size of the panel should be based on having all perspectives on the research topic adequately represented (p. 1490). In some cases, this could mean using very large panels; in other cases, because of the specialized nature of the topic, very small panels may be appropriate.

Closely tied to the size of the panel are the criteria for member selection. Novakowski and Wellar (2008) listed a number of criteria that could be taken into consideration when determining the "expert" status of candidates. The potential criteria included advanced degrees, publications, work experience, professional affiliation, gender, ethnicity, and life-cycle stage. The criteria for selection will vary, depending on the topic of study. The size and selection of the panel are key in obtaining reliable outcomes, but so is the process in which the panel participates.

One of the key methodological features of the Delphi method that contributes to its reliability is the iterative process of knowledge development. The best results occur when panels move past exchanging beliefs and begin to "reveal the conceptual basis for those beliefs; the reasons, causes, rationale and the how and why of each participant's views" (Rotondi & Gustafson, 1996, p. 35). While the development of consensus is an important feature of the Delphi in that consensus of experts is an important feature of reliability, the process of the expert panel's developing a greater understanding of the research topic leads the informed consensus (Gibson & Miller, 1990; Williams & Webb, 1994). The Delphi method is a credible research method when careful attention is given to these methodological matters. This credibility is evident in the findings of a large and growing number of studies that seek to uncover new knowledge in a variety of disciplines ranging from public policy to education, health, and business.

Data Analysis

The literature demonstrated a variety of approaches to data analysis in various studies that used the Delphi method. The Delphi method can require the researcher to employ both quantitative and qualitative data analysis strategies, depending on the research design and the stage of the study. A typical Delphi will have open-ended questions in the first round that require qualitative analysis using content analysis techniques, with the end goal of generating questions to which the panel can respond with some type of scaled quantitative measure (Hasson, Keeney, & McKenna, 2000, pp. 1011-1012; Powell, 2003, p. 379).

The results of the second round are analyzed by the researcher using ranking or rating techniques, with the goal of showing the emergence of the most important ideas being surfaced by the panel. This information is then fed back to the panel in third and subsequent rounds for further refinement. The expert panel is asked to respond to the refined data. One of the strengths of this method is that panel members are allowed to refine or change their opinions as they interact with the information fed back from previous rounds (Hasson, Keeney, & McKenna, 2000, p. 1010). This dynamic allows experts to build and refine their understanding of the research topic, leading to the best possible conclusion because the best people are collaborating on the best solution. This process continues until the researcher feels the panel has arrived at some type of consensus on the issue being studied.

The literature revealed a variety of views on the number of rounds that must be used in a Delphi study. The typical advice and practice indicated that two rounds are the minimum, with some researchers suggesting that up to five rounds may be necessary (Critcher & Gladstone, 1998, p. 432; Gibson & Miller, 1990, p. 36; Olshfski & Joseph, 1991, p. 298; Powell, 2003, p. 378). Keeney et al. (2006) gave helpful advice regarding completion by suggesting that the achievement of consensus or the lack of change in responses should determine the number of rounds required in a

Delphi study (p. 207). The difficulty for the researcher with this perspective lies in the fact that researchers most often must determine their methodology ahead of time. The flexibility to add rounds may not be present; ending the study sooner than anticipated would present fewer challenges.

A key question in any Delphi study is the level of consensus the researcher desires to achieve among the members of the panel. The Delphi method has no prescribed level of consensus (Powell, 2003, p. 379). Keeney et al. (2006) suggest that 75% should be the minimal level of consensus, but admit that there is no scientific basis for this number (p. 210). Most often the measurement of consensus entails the use of some type of descriptive or inferential statistics to determine the central tendencies (Hasson, Keeney, & McKenna, 2000, p. 379). Consensus entails a predetermined percentage of the expert panel agreeing that given data point or points have equal or similar value as they relate to the research question. This criterion assumes that the opinions of the experts will change based on their interaction with the material circulated through the rounds. This may or may not be a realistic expectation, depending on the makeup of the panel and the research topic.

In light of the challenges surrounding consensus as a measure of results, Goodman (1987) argued that stability in the responses over subsequent rounds is more important than consensus (p. 373). This assertion acknowledges that a panel of experts exploring a given research question may not come to a place of agreement. This result, according to Goodman, may be a valid outcome of the study.

Populations and Sampling

The research questions being considered in this study necessitated the use of a sampling technique that allowed the researcher to draw from a population that had the necessary background and understanding of the research topic. For this reason, purposive sampling was used to establish the population for this study (Patton, 2002, p. 230). The details of the methodology are discussed in greater detail in subsequent sections.

Preliminary Survey

The Preliminary Survey was sent to member organizations of the Nonprofit Association of Oregon (NAO). The NAO is an outgrowth of The Technical Assistance for Community Services (TACS), which began in 1977 with the mandate of providing training, consulting, and other professional services to community-based organizations (http://www.tacs.org/about_us). NAO is comprised of more than 400 member organizations and more than 100 individual members (http://www.tacs.org/non profit_association_of_oregon/about_nao). The NAO aids member organizations by making efforts to:

a) Increase capacity: Gain knowledge, training, and resources for fundraising, marketing, technical assistance, personnel management, and governance

b) Save money: Receive discounts on online giving tools, website templates, TACS trainings, and more

c) Advocate effectively: Track state and national topics and advance critical policy issues affecting the sector

d) Foster leadership and collaboration: Share best practices and create strategic partnerships that expand services and support

e) Achieve excellence: Honor standards of practice and accountability that advance the sector and help you realize your mission (http://www.tacs.org/nonprofit _association_of_oregon/about_nao)

The Preliminary Survey was sent to NAO member organizations that fit the profile of being a social sector nonprofit organization. A social sector nonprofit organization was defined as an organization that provides for the needs of the "deprived, neglected, or handicapped children and youth, the needy, elderly, the mentally ill and developmentally disabled and disadvantaged adults. These services include daycare, counseling, job training, child protection, foster care, residential treatment, homemakers, rehabilitation, and sheltered workshops" (Smith, 2002, p. 153). This study did not look at professional associations, groups that focus on the arts, religious organizations, or educational institutions.

The purpose of the Preliminary survey was twofold: first, to assess whether the organization does indeed meet the criteria of being a social service organization as outlined above; and second, to determine whether there was someone in the organization who met the criteria for participation in the Delphi panel and was willing to participate. The results of the Preliminary survey were used in the formation of the Delphi panel which engaged with the research questions.

The Delphi Panel

The expert panel needed to be large enough to represent a variety of perspectives related to the nonprofit sector in the state of Oregon, yet small enough so that the process was manageable and effective. Novakowski and Wellar (2008) recommend that the size of the panel be sufficient to allow for all perspectives on a topic be represented (pp. 1489-1491). For this reason, I determined that representations on the panel needed to be drawn from organization executives, nonprofit board members, and an educator in the field of nonprofit management.

Participants from the Preliminary survey who met the criteria for participation and indicate an interest were considered for the panel. The criteria for participation on the Delphi panel was influenced by Powell's (2003) criteria for panel members. Powell felt that a panel should be comprised in such a way as to reflect the breadth of current knowledge and practice on the topic and be more heterogeneous than homogenous (p. 379). With these considerations in mind, I established the following criteria:

1. Participants on the Delphi panel have at least five years of experience or practice in their given role with a social sector nonprofit organization.
2. No organization can have more than one individual on the panel.
3. The panel should have at least 10 members, but no more than 20.
4. Additional Delphi panel members may also be obtained by using the snowball technique, especially if there is

an obvious need for a particular perspective as outlined above to be represented on the Delphi panel.

5. Balance in race and gender of the panel would be helpful but would be considered as secondary to the role and experience of the individual.

These criteria guided the selection process for the Delphi panel. The result was a panel comprised of experts with experience in the nonprofit social sector and the knowledge that comes with time that enabled them to respond to the research question.

Instrumentation and Data Collection

The Preliminary Survey

The data collection for this study was done in two phases: the Preliminary survey and the Delphi panel. The Preliminary survey served to identify potential Delphi panel members, as well as gather a limited amount of basic information on the nonprofit organizations participating. The population for the Preliminary survey was composed of the organizational members who are part of the Nonprofit Association of Oregon (NOA). The Preliminary survey consisted of closed and open-ended questions intended to gather demographic information on the current leaders of NOA organizations, to acquire basic information on the organizations themselves, and to solicit participation in the Delphi panel. The demographic information gathered assisted in establishing the suitability of the willing respondent for participation in the Delphi panel.

The Preliminary survey instrument was adapted from a preliminary survey used by Holmes (2005) for a study using a similar methodology to study competencies for emerging practice in occupational therapy. The changes required rewording questions, adding questions to aid in the qualification of Delphi panelists, and including open-ended questions regarding the current challenges for nonprofit organizations. Where possible, the order and question type was left intact. The revised instrument was reviewed and then field tested by individuals with involvement in and knowledge of the nonprofit sector (see Appendix A).

The Delphi Panel

Round One

The format of the first round of a Delphi study is the subject of debate among researchers. Some suggest that the questions in the first round must be unstructured (Hasson, Keeney, & McKenna, 2000, p. 1011; Martino, 1983, p. 18; Powell, 2003, p. 378) to insure that the researcher is not in any way influencing the outcomes. However, Powell (2003) does note studies that have employed semi-structured or structured questions in the first round that drew on literature related to the topic at hand (p. 378). I chose to begin with an unstructured question to avoid issues related to bias and research subjectivity that can be introduced by producing lists of competencies from the literature for the panel to review. The Delphi model was built around open-ended questions to ensure that the input from the expert panel was minimally influenced by the researcher. This approach allowed me to do evaluations and comparisons of the results from the Delphi panel with competency models produced in other studies without having to be concerned about questions related to the panel's being influenced by the structure given in the first round.

Each member of the Delphi panel received via email, the following documents: a brief overview of the study, definitions of key terms and ideas, instructions for the questionnaire, and the questionnaire itself. Submission of the documents by email was encouraged. The open-ended question asked in Round one was: In your opinion, what are the skills, knowledge, traits, motives, and self-concept/self-understanding that are essential for executive-level leaders in nonprofit, social services organizations? The instructions encouraged the panelists to give their responses in a format that was most conducive to disclosing as much information as possible. Panelists had the opportunity to narrative or a bullet format. They were encouraged to include explanations for their answers. The explanations are a critical component in understanding the reasoning of each panelist, which were helpful not only for me, but also for the other panelists as they moved into the subsequent rounds. The instructions also encouraged the panelists to think as broadly as possible about the role of a leader in the social service sector, moving beyond what the leader does to include that person's qualities and traits as a person.

A reminder email was sent to all panelists who have not yet responded two weeks after the initial information pack was sent. The panel's feedback regarding the Round one question was analyzed and compiled to form the basis of Round two in the

Delphi. The detail of the analysis will be discussed in the data analysis section of this chapter.

Round Two

The second round of the Delphi consisted of a questionnaire developed from the first-round responses and instructions for the expert panel. In this round, the panel was asked to respond to the results gathered in the first round by assigning a type of ranking to the items collected. It was the intent of the researcher to follow the competency categories or clusters as outlined by Spencer and Spencer (1993) as closely as possible. This allowed in the creation of a framework from which to better evaluate and organize the data submitted by the panel. Categories were added to accommodate the panel responses in the first round. Panelists were asked to give a brief explanation for the ranking they assign.

In addition to ranking items, the expert panel was asked to assign a weight to each item in the list. The item with lowest importance was assigned a 10 on a scale of 10 -100. Each item was assigned a weighting that was used to further investigate the importance of each item relative to its ranking by all panelists. A follow-up email was sent two weeks after the package of the material was sent, encouraging a timely response.

Round Three

In the third and final round of the Delphi, the expert panel was asked to respond to the results of the second round. The second round results showed how the competencies identified in earlier rounds were ranked and weighted by the group as a whole. Each participant was sent a summary of his or her own rankings for comparison purposes. The panel members had opportunity to review the rankings and written comments. Participants were instructed to rank the results again in light of information gained from other panel members. The experts were free to change their responses from the previous round or have them remain the same.

Throughout the research portion of this study, electronic communication and methods of gathering results were used as much as possible. This method was chosen for two primary reasons: it allowed for quicker turnaround time, which ideally helped to bolster the participation rate; and it reduced the amount of data entry required, saving time and reduced the possibility of errors. All information and other communication exchanged among the group members used the blind copy field to ensure that panelists cannot identify one another. I did not disclose the identity of the panelists to those on the panel or in the results of the study. See Appendix B for a summary of the various stages of the research project.

Data Analysis

The research project had both quantitative and qualitative data elements. SPSS was used for analysis of the numerical data elements, and NVivo 8 was used for the qualitative responses from the Delphi panel. A detailed discussion of the analysis process follows.

Preliminary Survey

The responses to the questions asked in the preliminary survey had quantitative and qualitative elements. The quantitative elements were analyzed using SPSS to measure the descriptive statistics and central tendencies. This data was found in responses to various questions throughout the survey. Some open-ended questions were added to gather background information on the leaders, their roles, and the organizations in which they serve. This information was gathered for two reasons: First, it was used to help develop a better understanding of nonprofits in the Pacific Northwest; and second, it was used to help qualify potential experts for the Delphi panel. The information from the Preliminary was compiled and analyzed using NVivo 8 when drawn from an open-ended question.

The Delphi Panel

The desired outcome of this study was to generate a list of proposed competencies for executive leaders in the social service organizations in the nonprofit sector. The Delphi panel members submitted responses to an open-ended question, and in later rounds, quantitative data from the panel in the form of rankings and weighting of items was collected as well. The analysis of data from the Delphi panel required the use of SPSS, NVivo 8 and Excel.

The data from Round one of the Delphi panel was from a single open-ended question that required qualitative analysis. The data was examined to discover common themes and to discover how they may fit with the Spencer and Spencer (1993) competence model. The Spencer and Spencer model contained six clusters in which 21 competencies were included. The clusters were Achievement & action, Helping and human service, Impact and influence, Managerial, Cognitive, and Personal effectiveness.

The responses from the panel were summarized and then formatted as a questionnaire for Round two. The panel was asked to rank each item in order of importance and to weight each item.

The quantitative results from the Round two questionnaires were analyzed using SPSS. The median rank, median weighted score, and the standard deviation of both were calculated. This information was part of the information package circulated to the panel for the third and final round. The information included the definitions, instructions for the third round, and the questionnaire itself, which consisted largely of data from Round two.

The questionnaire contained the analyzed data from Round two. The items were listed by cluster or category in descending order of importance as ranked by the panel of experts. The standard deviation for the importance score, along with the average weighted score and deviation, were included for review by the panel.

The results from round three were analyzed using Excel. Evaluating the results from this third and final round included the important step of discerning the level of stability in the results between rounds two and three. Goodman (1987) noted that while most Delphi studies pursue consensus among the panel, having a division of opinion can be a valid result as long as there is stability in the responses. The expectation was that this study would result in a consensus among the panel members regarding the competencies needed in social service nonprofit organizations. However, data stability can validate a result that has a lower level of consensus, as well as serving as a signal that further rounds of inquiry are not needed. Once responses have stabilized less new information will be gained, making subsequent rounds less productive.

One of the key elements in the final round was using the weighted scores to understand the value of one item relative to another as determined by the group, which was a point made by Clark and Friedman (1982) in their study on mental health treatment outcomes (p. 91) that utilized a weighting system to better understand the relative value of each item. Multi-attribute utilities (MAU) have been used in a variety of fields and studies. MAU give a method of calculating values of different options available to determine which would be of the greatest importance (Cabrera & Raju, 2001, p. 98; Mussi, 1999, p. 88). The standardized weighted scores were calculated using the same method employed by Holmes (2005), Clark and Friedman (1982), and Lagoudis, Lalwani, and Naim (2006). This method entailed summing the weighted values for each item and dividing each single item weight by that sum. The result showed the proportion of the value of each item relative to the category as a whole. The standardized weight value coupled with ranking gave a much clearer understanding of the importance of a given competency relative to the others.

Limitations

This study had limitations in terms of the applicability of results due to the regional nature and size of the population used in the study. The results of the study will be helpful to nonprofit social service organizations in the Pacific Northwest as they seek to recruit, train, and develop executive level leaders for this type of organization. The study outcomes may inform, but should not be taken as representative of, the competencies of leaders in other types of nonprofit organizations. It may also be possible that the competencies identified will be regional in nature and should not be applied to nonprofit social service organizations in other parts of the United States.

While the sample size employed in this study falls within the established parameters for Delphi studies, the intent of a Delphi study is to explore an area in which there is little or no research. This study should be viewed as a starting point for further research into competency models for nonprofit organizations. Further study in this area could lead to the validation of models that could be more widely applied and used in the development of leaders in a variety of nonprofit organizations.

Ethical Considerations

This research proposal was reviewed by the Gonzaga University Institutional Review Board to ensure that ethical standards and practices were in place prior to the collection of data. The two different phases of this research entail different ethical considerations.

While the simple act of returning a survey can imply consent on the part of the participant, the researcher also outlined for the participants how the data collected will be used. This information was included as part of the instructions that accompany the preliminary survey. The preliminary survey did not ask for personal information, but rather focused on the nonprofit organization and the participants' relationship with that organization.

Delphi Survey

Social science researchers must do all they can to protect those participating in research from harm. The principle of informed consent for research dictates that participants voluntarily take part in a study with a full understanding of the possible risks and benefits (Babbie, 2004, p. 64). To this end, a consent form for the Delphi panel members was prepared that outlined the purpose of the study, the procedures that were followed, and the expectations of panel members, along with other considerations and rights.

One of the strengths of the Delphi method is the freedom of expression participants have because of their anonymity (Gibson & Miller, 1990, p. 35; Powell, 2003, p. 377; Williams & Webb, 1994, p. 181). Participants were informed that they have the right to withdraw at any time, that their communication with the researcher will remain confidential, that their responses to the questions will remain anonymous, and that they may choose to not answer a question or questions. The participants also had the right to view the results of the study. The responses to second and third round questions were returned anonymously to ensure that the panel members felt free to express their opinions related to the questions.

Conclusion

Even though this research project proposal contains two main parts, the Preliminary survey and the Delphi survey, the research questions were answered primarily from the data collected in the Delphi survey. Based on the literature and previous studies, the methodology outlined did result in the acquisition of valuable information that not only answered the proposed research questions, but also could guide future research in this area of leadership development for nonprofit organizations.

Chapter Four

Results

The purpose of this study was to identify a competency model for executive leaders of social service organizations within the nonprofit sector. This chapter presents results of data collection addressing three research questions: a) What competencies are needed for executives to lead effectively in the social service organization in the nonprofit sector? b) How do the competencies identified by leaders in a particular nonprofit sector compare with competencies lists formulated for similar roles in other sectors? and c) Can a set of competencies unique to nonprofit organizations be identified for use in recruitment and development of nonprofit leaders?

The research design included two main components. An invitation to participate in a Preliminary Survey was sent to the membership of the Nonprofit Association of Oregon (NAO); general information regarding the respondents' nonprofit was collected along with details regarding the current challenges faced by nonprofits in the Northwest. Participants were given an opportunity to indicate their interest in participating in the second component, a Delphi panel, which developed the competency model for leaders of nonprofit, social service agencies. The results of the Preliminary Survey are presented first, followed by the results of the three rounds of responses from the Delphi panel.

Preliminary Survey Results

The Preliminary Survey consisted of 18 questions that requested information regarding the respondents' background with the nonprofit sector, training for their current role in a nonprofit organization, and general information on the nonprofit organization itself. An invitation to participate was included in the January 2011 e-newsletter published by NOA. This e-newsletter is sent to approximately 8,000 addresses. A reminder was included in the February edition of the newsletter. The survey closed March 20, 2011. This effort resulted in 22 completed surveys. This rate of return is too low for the results to be viewed as representative of the population. However, the descriptive elements were compiled to see what may be learned regarding the current state of nonprofits in the Pacific Northwest.

Roles of Preliminary Survey Participants

Of the 22 respondents to the survey, 17 were paid staff, one was a volunteer, three were board members, and one individual noted no current involvement. The job titles for those who responded are found in Table 4. Executive Directors made up the largest group of respondents (11) followed by managers (5).

The respondents as a whole possessed a great deal of experience within the nonprofit sector. Board Members had the

Table 4: Summary of Respondent Roles & Time in Nonprofit Sector

Role/Job Title	# of Responses	% of Total	Average Years as Paid Staff	Average Years on Board	Average Years Volunteer
Board Member	2	9%	-	32	35
Executive Director	11	50%	30	11	16
Director/Manager	5	23%	19.3	3	2
Vice President	1	4.5%	-	3	3
No Response	3	13.5%	-	-	-

most volunteer experience averaging 35 years with Executive Directors having the most experience as paid staff averaging 30 years. This means that 59% of the respondents to the Preliminary Survey had at least 30 years of experience in the nonprofit sector. One can surmise, based on the years of experience, that the respondents have a good understanding of the opportunities and challenges associated with the nonprofit sector.

The organizations represented in the Preliminary Survey serve a broad range of clientele and causes, mostly in the Pacific Northwest, although one organization works in Tanzania. The services provided included victim support services, crisis intervention, education for parents and children, medical services, advocacy, pet adoptions, art education, and environmental education. Those served by these organizations were from every age category, with a focus on those who would be classified as economically disadvantaged.

Factors Contributing to Development

The survey asked the population to indicate the significance (1=very significant, 2=significant, 3=somewhat significant, or 4=not significant) of the listed items to the knowledge and skills required in their current position. Thirteen responses to this question were collected. This number is not adequate to make any type of generalization to a greater population, but does present some insight into how this group of leaders viewed various means of gaining skills and knowledge pertaining to leading in the nonprofit sector.

The index used to compile the results of this question was very significant =1; significant= 2, somewhat significant = 3; and not significant = 4. This group of respondents rated interaction with colleagues (M=1.15, SD=0.38) as being the most significant of the factors listed (see Table 5). The high mean score and low standard deviation confirm the highest importance of this particular factor among all respondents. The low standard deviation points to a high degree of agreement among the respondents. Interaction with colleagues is followed by on-the-job training (M=1.50, SD=0.67), seminars or conferences (M=1.58, SD=0.90), and previous roles (M=1.64, SD=0.92). It is interesting to note that the top four factors tend toward opportunities that allow leaders to quickly gain knowledge and skills that can be applied to their immediate context. The focus seems to be on the ability to quickly learn or glean ideas and solutions that can be implemented with minimal development.

Table 5 also illustrates that among the respondents, more formal opportunities for skill and knowledge development are viewed as less significant than opportunities that have more personal interaction. The lowest-ranked opportunities included undergraduate education (M=2.46, SD=0.88), formal mentoring (M=2.36, SD=1.21), and selected courses (M=2.15, SD=1.14).

Table 5: Factors Contributing to Respondent's Development for Current Role

Contribution Type	Average	Std Dev
Interaction with colleagues	1.15	0.38
On-the-job training	1.50	0.67
Seminars or conferences	1.58	0.90
Previous roles in nonprofit organizations	1.64	0.92
Graduate education	2.00	1.15
Informal mentoring	2.08	0.95
Selected courses	2.15	1.14
Formal mentoring	2.36	1.21
Undergraduate education	2.46	0.88

Graduate education (M=2.00, SD=1.15) was ranked highest among those items requiring a more formal educational setting. Though there was no opportunity for respondents to give explanations for their rankings, I speculate that the reason for the high ranking of graduate education versus other formal approaches is that graduate courses tend to be smaller in size and more focused in their content than undergraduate courses. This arrangement may foster the notion of being more helpful in the development of the skills and knowledge for a nonprofit leader.

Overall, these results suggest that the respondents viewed opportunities that have more personal interaction with colleagues who have current experience in the sector as more valuable to their development than more formal, theoretical opportunities that may be available. The implication for those involved in the development of nonprofit leaders is that they would do well to explore ways of allowing the potential leaders to interact with one another and focus learning opportunities on immediate and practical needs within the sector.

Challenges Faced

The respondents were also asked to share what they viewed as the most significant challenges facing their organizations. Twelve people responded to this question. Funding was mentioned in some form by eight of the 12. This does not come as much of a surprise, considering that the timing of the survey corresponded with an economic recession. Challenges related to human resource issues were noted by five respondents. The human resource issues mentioned included dealing with staff transition, having adequate staff to meet the demand for services, and the development of training programs for staff and board.

There is an element of interconnectedness in the challenges mentioned: Inadequate funding leading to inadequate staffing places more stress on existing staff to do more in the face of rising demand. Executive Directors and managers are so busy with the immediate issues of funding and demand for services that little time is left for staff development and organizational planning. One respondent stated her challenge by explaining that there is: "no time for upper level admin staff to adequately manage and train newer staff or deal with low performers. No position for human resources so hiring is extremely difficult".

Additional Training

The Preliminary Survey also asked for input on the type of additional training or education that would be most helpful. The results were analyzed using NVivo, resulting in the emergence of three main areas: board development and motivation; mentoring and personnel development; and financial matters, with grant writing and budgeting being specifically noted. The topics of public speaking, mediation, and understanding of federal and state and laws, along with grant writing, were also mentioned. Two of the three main areas have a very strong focus on the management and development side of leadership.

These are individuals with a good deal of education. Nine of the 13 who answered the question regarding their own educational background indicated having completed at least a bachelor's degree, with six having master's degrees. However, they still feel the need to develop and improve their skills in areas that are major components of the executive leader role. The areas mentioned for further education—board development, personnel development, and finances—do relate closely to the challenges listed, which included finances, HR issues, and working with their boards. The alignment of these two areas suggests validity in the findings. These items regularly present challenges and opportunities for those who assist nonprofits to meet the perceived needs of nonprofit leaders.

Staffing Levels

The survey also requested information concerning the staffing of the nonprofit organizations. Table 6 displays the results of this question, showing the number of organizations that reported having staff in one of the four categories. The total staffing reported by all respondents was also included in the table.

The results revealed that within the organizations reporting, the greatest number of staff were in the part-time volunteer category. The smallest category was full-time volunteers,

Table 6: Summary of Organizational Staffing by Type (Count of Organizations and Total Staffing)

	Paid Full-Time	Volunteer Full-Time	Paid Part-Time	Volunteer Part-Time
# of Organizations	11	3	11	12
Total Staffing	225	6	349	892

with the paid categories of staff (full & part-time) being close in number to one another. Two of the 13 organizations reported having no full-time paid staff. This information makes it clear that the nonprofit sector cannot survive without its volunteer workforce, which outnumbered the number of paid staff (full & part-time) by a margin of 574 to 898. The organizations surveyed for this study depend heavily on volunteers. This finding seems to support claims that Americans volunteer in large numbers in a variety of nonprofit organizations (Weitzman, Jalandoni, Lampkin, & Pollack, 2002, p. 21)

As previously noted, the small number of surveys completed makes it impossible to view the results as representative of a larger population. However, it should be noted that this group did clearly indicate some areas in which they feel the need to further develop their skills and expertise. These would represent areas of opportunity for those that support nonprofit organizations. In seeking to address these areas of perceived need, it should also be pointed out that those surveyed view interaction with colleagues as the most beneficial means of their own development. The results in Table 5 show that respondents rated interaction with colleagues, on-the-job training, and seminars or conferences as the most significant contributors to the knowledge and skills needed. It is apparent that nonprofit leaders have learned a great deal from one another. This factor should be a consideration in the planning of development and educational opportunities for nonprofit leaders. Venues and events where perceived needs can be addressed and opportunities are provided for interaction with colleagues would, based on the survey findings, be of value to nonprofit leaders. I suggest that further work is necessary with nonprofit leaders to corroborate the findings of the survey and the proposed format of development opportunities before developing an entire strategy. However, the results do provide a strong indication of the current challenges and needs facing nonprofit leaders in the Northwest.

The Delphi Panel Results

The Delphi panel was comprised of individuals who had at least five years of senior leadership experience with a social service agency in the nonprofit sector. Efforts were made to include panel members who came from different types of social service agencies and had varying points of contact. The panel included agency executives, board members, consultants to the sector, and one educator who regularly teaches in the field of nonprofit management. The Delphi panel members had an average of 18.6 years of experience in the nonprofit sector as paid staff, volunteers, and board members. Ten individuals from the Preliminary Survey indicated willingness to participate in the

Delphi panel. One of the individuals did not meet the criterion of serving in a social service agency and therefore was disqualified to serve on the panel. The remaining nine were sent additional information and the consent form for participation. Eight of the nine returned forms and were sent the material for Round One.

The size of the panel was further increased by inviting the participation of recommended individuals who fit the criteria. This move resulted in an additional five individuals being invited to participate. Four agreed to participate, submitted consent documents, and were sent the Round One materials. Two participants withdrew before completing the Round One Survey, leaving 10 participants who completed and submitted results. After Round One was completed, one more participant requested to withdraw.

Table 7 presents the employment and educational background of the Delphi Panel. The highest level of education achieved was reported. The panel contained seven senior-level leaders from nonprofit, social sector agencies, one educator,

Table 7: Employment and Educational Background of Delphi Panel

	Round One (n=10)	Round Two (n=9)	Round Three (n=8)
Job Title			
Faculty	1	1	1
Executive Director	5	5	4
Board Member	2	2	2
VP/President	2	1	1
Educational Background			
Doctoral Degree	1	1	1
Master's Degree	3	3	3
Bachelor's Degree	4	3	2
Less than Bachelor's	2	2	2

and two board members. This blend of personal experience and backgrounds allowed for a more well-rounded perspective on the competencies to be considered. Many of the panel members reported having previous or current involvement in more than one role in the sector, such as being paid staff in one organization as well as a board member for another organization. All but three had significant volunteer experience in the nonprofit sector.

Round One

The panel members provided feedback to an initial open-ended question that requested a listing of competencies they felt were important for leaders of the type of agency in which they serve. To provide more structure and guidance, panel members were asked to place their responses under one of five headings, with an option to include competencies outside these categories as well. The five headings were:

- Skills—What must the leader be able to do?
- Knowledge—What must the leader know?
- Traits—What personal characteristics contribute to role success?
- Motives—What motivates the leader? What causes an individual to fully engage in their work?
- Self-concept/self-understandings—How does the leader view self, his or her role, and others?

The five categories above were provided as a means of helping the panel to think as broadly as possible about the open-ended question and to assist in compiling the results from the first round by giving working definition to provide a common understanding of the categories. The open-ended question the panel responded to was "In your opinion, what are the skills, knowledge, traits, motives, and self-concept/self-understanding that are essential for executive-level leaders in nonprofit, social services organizations?" A complete set of the instructions and materials for Round One are included in Appendix C.

A content analysis was completed for this question. The responses given by the panel covered a wide range of topics and ideas. The five categories given to the panel with the Round One question were used in the analysis and compilation of the results. NVIVO was used in the initial assessment of the results from Round One. Once the basic areas under each category were established, the results were grouped and refined without use of NVIVO. Any duplicate entries were removed.

In developing the competencies, the actual wording from the responses was used as much as possible to name and define the actual competencies. The result was a list of 30 different competencies divided under five categories.

Skills

The first category under which competencies were developed was the category of "Skills." This category was defined for the panel as being what the leader must be able to do. The responses under the Skills category were compiled into the following random list of skill-related competencies:

- Communication/Listening
- Problem Solving
- Building/Managing a Team

- Empathy/Compassion
- Organizational Planning & Development
- Financial Management & Development
- Respect for People
- Relationships Outside the Organization
- Decision Making
- Leadership Perspective

Based on the panel's responses, 10 competencies were developed under the Skills category. These items represent a full third of the total number of competencies identified. They ranged from skills that are very practical in nature, such as listening and communication skills, to other items that are more abstract and seemingly tied more closely to personal values. This latter category would include items such as respect for people, empathy, and the skill of having a leadership perspective. These items have obvious outward manifestations, but could be viewed as springing from a particular set of deeply held personal values. This is not to say that the other competencies have no basis in personal values, but rather that some skills, like empathy, flow more naturally as a by-product of values that place importance on the individual.

Knowledge

The next set of competencies identified from the Delphi panel's results came under the category of "Knowledge," which was explained as consisting of what a leader must know. The line between the Skills and the Knowledge competencies was at times difficult to create. In the end, I determined that while some of the competencies in these two categories could be interchanged, for the sake of the study, as much as possible I sought to respect the results of the panel. Five competencies were identified from the Round One results. They were:

- Board Function & Development
- Information/Learning Skills
- Legal & Operational Requirements
- Conflict Resolution & Mediation
- Spokesperson & Cheerleader

Although many of the competencies listed under the Knowledge category have an obvious knowledge component, the effective application of this knowledge also requires that a leader have good interpersonal skills. Knowing how a board ought to function and putting this awareness into practice can be two very different things. The best nonprofit leaders have both the knowledge and the interpersonal skills to bring about positive and productive functioning of boards and their organizations.

The one competency that fit the knowledge definition very well was the Information and Learning Skills competency. Multiple members of the Delphi panel mentioned items that highlighted their belief that nonprofit leaders must possess the willingness to learn, the desire to gather information, and the ability to learn on their own. They must also know how to use technology to further the goals of their organization.

Traits

The Delphi panelists were asked to list the personal characteristics they thought contributed to the success of a nonprofit leader. The term "personal characteristics" was intentionally left undefined to allow for the panel members' autonomy in their responses. This category generated the most overall responses and had the greatest breadth of competencies found in any category. This is likely the case because the panel members all had slightly different ideas about what constituted a personal characteristic. A varied and rich perspective emerged from these materials gathered. The competencies compiled from the responses were:

- Team Orientation
- Patience/Perseverance
- Personal Traits
- Work/Professional Traits
- Interpersonal Skills/Traits

The results of this category differ from the others slightly in that two of the competencies could be viewed as stand-alone competencies (Team Orientation and Patience), while the remaining three represent a set of traits related to spheres in which leaders operate, often concurrently. These categories are based loosely on the expression of the traits, though the lines are best viewed in shades of gray, not black and white. The traits listed by the panel could be viewed, in some instances, as being interchangeable among the competencies.

The final decision on placement was made based on the context of the panelists' responses. Any bias on my part that may have been introduced in this evaluation and compilation process was mitigated by allowing the actual comments to define the competency heading created. Although I chose the wording for the

171

competency labels, the definitions were drawn from the submission of the panel, and the panel members were able to view those definitions in subsequent rounds.

The most interesting thing about these competencies is that they are based more on the person of the leader than previous competencies. Skills and knowledge can be learned or acquired, but many of the competencies identified in the Traits category (i.e. patience, fairness, flexible, consist) are anchored in the person of the leader. Some aspects can be learned, but this is less true of the items in this category than of those listed under skills or knowledge.

Motives

The next category given to the Delphi panel for consideration was the category of Motives defined as "What motivates the leader?" and "What causes an individual to fully engage in his or her work?" The competencies identified by the panel were compiled into six competencies that encapsulated the submissions of the Delphi panel. The competencies were as follows:

- Commitment to the Mission/Purpose
- Compensation
- Meaningful Work/Seeing Results
- Personal Values
- Relationship with Colleagues
- Enjoyment of Administrative Work

Most of the resulting competencies would fit within a competency framework. The one item that is a poor fit within the competency frame is compensation. Compensation, while it is a motive, is not a competency. However, it was decided to leave this item in the list for the second round to observe how the Delphi panel would treat this item in the rankings.

As a whole, this category is not identified in other competency models, although specific competencies in this category are evident. Competencies such as commitment to the mission/purpose, meaningful work/seeing results, and relationship with colleagues all have parallels in the model outlined by Spencer and Spencer (1993, p. 25 - 88). Compensation, while not a competency as defined by this study, is nonetheless a motivating factor. Later results show compensation to be of lesser value when compared with other competencies from the Delphi panel.

Self-Concept

The fifth and final category given to the Delphi panel was that of Self-concept, defined as how the leader views himself or herself, his or her role, and others. The responses were compiled into the following four competencies:

- Humble
- Takes Responsibility for the Development & Success of the Organization
- Outcomes/Results Driven
- Self-assured/Confident

The results from the panel correspond with and have similarities to competencies identified by both Boyatzis (1982) and Spencer and Spencer (1993). The exception is humility. While humility is not found in most competency models, Collins (2005) highlights humility as being one of the key components of what he classified as a "Level Five Leader" (p. 142). Collins views humility, along with professional will, as being the hallmark of a Level Five leader, whom he views as being capable of taking an organization to the next level. While humility is not found in traditional competency models, it is a factor that should be considered based on the more recent work by Collins.

The panelists were also given the option of providing responses in an open category if they felt a competency they chose to include did not fit the listed categories. The feedback placed in this category was limited and consisted largely of commentary on the initial question. The comments are listed below.

> I don't think it matters if you are a leader of a social service organization, a small business, a corporation, or an arts non-profit. I think good business leadership skills transcend industry boundaries.

> Much depends on the size of the organization. In smaller agencies, the leader is responsible for doing much of the service work in addition to the larger overview piece. In larger agencies, the leader needs different skills such as political savvy.

These comments highlight a couple of important points. First, business skills are necessary and applicable in any type of organization; and second, the skill-set of the leader may need to vary depending on the size of the organization. The results of the first round support the first point, since there are a number of competencies in the results from the panel that are general leadership or management skills needed by any executive regardless of the sector in which he or she works. Though the size of the organization may indeed affect the competencies required of the leader, this study did not use this as a separate variable or take it into consideration when analyzing the results.

Round Two

The results from Round One were compiled and organized using the same five categories from the first round. A total of 30 competencies were identified across the five categories. A complete set of the instructions and other materials for Round Two are found in Appendices D and E. The Delphi panelists were asked to review the compiled list and suggest additional items they deemed necessary. The panel was also asked to numerically rank the items in each category, with one being the most important, and continuing until each item was ranked.

In addition to ranking the items, the Delphi Panel was asked to assign a weighting to each item. The weighting assists in understanding the relative importance of the items compared with one another within each category. The weighting provided additional data that allowed insight into the actual interval the panelist may have intended when using an ordinal ranking method. Each category was ranked 10-100, with panelists being asked to start with their least important item at 10 and to work from that point up to 100 without duplicate numbers.

Nine of the 10 panelists returned their surveys, giving a 90% return rate.

Ranking by Category

The group means and standard deviation for rank and weighting by category are presented in tables 8-12. During the analysis, the rank and weighting group means and the standard deviation were determined for each competency in each category. A lower mean group rank indicated a greater importance of the particular competency. A higher mean group weighting score meant a particular item was perceived as having higher importance. The group weighting score also provided a greater understanding of the intervals between ranked items. All competencies in the tables are in ranked order, beginning with the competency of greatest importance and progressing to those with the lowest ranking.

Table 8 presents the ten items in the Skills category. The

Table 8: Round Two Results for Skills (Rank and Weight Group Means and Standard Deviation)

	Mean Group Rank	Standard Deviation	Mean Group Weight	Standard Deviation
Building/Managing a Team	3.00	1.50	75.56	20.64
Communication/Listening	3.33	2.40	79.44	18.78
Organizational Planning & Development	4.22	3.11	58.11	34.62
Financial Management & Development	4.89	2.20	60.33	22.29
Leadership Perspective	5.00	3.00	59.44	29.11
Respect for People	5.56	3.28	61.56	25.51
Problem Solving	6.11	2.15	57.00	24.79
Decision Making	6.56	2.51	34.89	27.79
Empathy/Compassion	7.67	2.06	46.56	27.03
Relationships outside the organization	8.67	1.50	36.11	31.00

results gathered from the Delphi panel in Round One were used to create and define these competencies.

The mean group rank of the most important item was 3.00, with a standard deviation of 1.50. The second competency had a mean score of 3.33. In looking at the standard deviation scores, a 1.50 suggests a high degree of consensus among the panel members regarding building and managing a team being the most important competency in this category. The weighting for this item is also high, though not as high as the weighting for communication and listening. This incongruence in the results is not large (75.56 versus 79.44) and not unusual in the early rounds of Delphi studies. The Delphi method allows the panel to address these types of irregularities in subsequent rounds.

The next five items in the list are all fairly close in ranking and weighting. A significant gap in ranking and weighting exists between competency two (communication) and competency three (organizational planning). Another gap exists between problem solving and decision making. The results show that the Delphi panel clearly identified two competencies as being most important, followed by a grouping of five that were secondary, and finally three competencies in this category that were seemingly regarded by the panel as being of less importance. The low standard deviation on the ranked score for Relationships outside the organization shows a high level of agreement on the low ranking of this competency.

Table 9 presents the mean rank, weighted group mean, and standard deviation for the five competencies identified by the panel for the category of Knowledge.

Table 9: Round Two Results for Knowledge (Rank and Weight Group Means and Standard Deviation)

	Mean Group Rank	Standard Deviation	Mean Group Weight	Standard Deviation
Information/ Learning Skills	2.22	1.72	68.11	28.91
Board Function & Development	2.44	0.88	72.67	23.47
Legal & Operational Requirements	3.11	1.69	57.78	38.49
Spokesperson/Cheerleader	3.33	1.12	54.00	28.20
Conflict Resolution & Mediation	3.89	1.17	56.22	32.13

Information and Learning Skills had a mean group rank of 2.22 with a standard deviation of 1.72. Although this competency ranked first by group mean, the weighting score placed it second. Only .22 separated the top two competencies in the group rankings, and just over four points separated them in the weightings. These results from the Delphi panel show these two items as clearly being the most important of the five competencies in this category. The weighting for the five items in this group falls roughly into two groupings: the top two competencies and the bottom three, with an obvious break between the two in terms of both the rankings and the weighting score.

Conflict resolution and mediation had the highest ranked group mean score, meaning it was viewed as being the least important. The lower standard deviation of 1.17 indicates agreement of the panelists on the placement. Overall, the standard deviation scores for the Knowledge category are lower than for the Skills category, likely because there are fewer competencies (five as opposed to 10) in the Knowledge category.

Table 10: Round Two Results for Traits (Rank and Weight Group Means and Standard Deviation)

	Mean Group Rank	Standard Deviation	Mean Group Weight	Standard Deviation
Interpersonal Skills/Traits	2.00	1.22	81.67	11.06
Work/Professional Traits	2.33	1.32	74.56	21.92
Team Orientation	3.22	0.67	67.67	25.06
Personal Traits	3.44	1.67	50.33	35.44
Patience/Perseverance	4.00	1.32	38.78	31.34

The group results for the Traits category are shown in Table 11. The group mean results and mean group weighting are parallel throughout, meaning that the ranked order and the weighting match.

Interpersonal Skills and Traits had a group rank mean of 2.00 and mean group weighting of 81.67, placing it first in this category. The rankings continue lower, with Patience and Perseverance having the lowest-ranked mean score of 4.00 and a weighting of 38.78. Team Orientation has the lowest standard deviation on the ranking and weighting, indicating a high degree of panel consensus on the placement of this competency. There was also an observable trend: The lower weighting scores had higher standard deviations, which signals a higher degree of variation in the attitude of the panel members regarding that particular item. An example concerns the competency of Patience and Perseverance. The average weighting is 38.78 with a standard deviation of 31.34. The responses from the panel varied greatly, as is shown by the high standard deviation score.

Table 11: Round Two Results for Motives (Rank and Weight Groups Means and Standard Deviation)

	Mean Group Rank	Standard Deviation	Mean Group Weight	Standard Deviation
Commitment to Mission/Purpose	1.33	0.50	90.33	11.22
Meaningful Work/Seeing Results	2.11	1.05	80.00	15.99
Relationships w/ Colleagues	4.00	1.22	56.67	23.72
Personal Values	4.11	1.05	58.67	22.51
Enjoyment of Administrative Work	4.22	1.56	38.56	30.35
Compensation	5.22	1.09	41.67	30.89

Table 11 contains the results for the Motive category of competencies from the Delphi panel. The top-ranked competency was Commitment to Mission with a mean group ranking of 1.33, followed closely by Meaningful Work with an average ranking of 2.11. The standard deviation for both of these competencies was low, suggesting a high level of consensus among the panel members. This agreement is also evidenced by the high group weighting score for these two items, along with low standard deviation showing agreement related to the weighting.

There was a nearly 2-point increase in the ranking between the second-ranked competency (Meaningful Work) and the third-ranked competency (Relationships with Colleagues). The lesser importance of the last four competencies relative to the first two is further seen in the corresponding decrease in the mean weighted score. The lowest-ranked item in this category was Compensation with a group ranking of 5.22. All rankings for this category would have been on a scale of 1-6.

The results of the last of the five categories, Self-concept/ Self-understanding, are presented in Table 12.

Table 12: Round Two Results for Self-concept/Self-understanding (Rank and Weight Groups Means and Standard Deviation)

	Mean Group Rank	Standard Deviation	Mean Group Weight	Standard Deviation
Take Responsibility for Development/Success of Organization	1.67	0.87	82.11	14.59
Outcomes Focus/Results Oriented	2.33	1.00	64.44	32.02
Self-assured/Confident/Self-aware	2.89	0.78	63.22	35.54
Humble	3.11	1.36	41.11	38.55

There were four competencies in the category, with Responsibility for Development/Success of the Organization attaining the highest ranking with a 1.67 and a standard deviation of .87. The mean group score was 82.11 with a standard deviation of 14.59. The results for this particular item point to a high level of consensus on the panel. The remaining items have increasing group rankings and decreasing group weighting scores. It should be noted that the group weight for items two and three are very close, suggesting that the panel viewed these items as being comparable in importance.

It is also worth noting that the final competency, Humility, had the lowest mean group weight (41.11), but also had a standard deviation nearly as large as the weighting. This shows a very wide dispersal on the weighting applied to this item by the panel. Subsequent rounds of the Delphi process can address these types of outliers in the data.

Top 15 Ranking

The Delphi panel members ranked what they assessed as the 15 most important competencies from the list of 30 competencies. The results are shown in Table 13; they are listed in order of greatest importance to least importance.

The methodology for creating the ranked order presented included two calculations. The first is a count of the number of votes a competency received. The results are shown in Table 13 under the heading of Count of Top 15 Selections. The second calculation, shown in column labeled Numerical Score, is the inverted sum of the individual rankings for each item. This configuration was chosen to factor in the level of the ranking itself, not just the fact that an item was ranked. The inverted numerical value was assigned by giving any item that was ranked 1 the value of 15; a ranking of 2 was given a 14. This was done for each item. This process allowed the value of the rankings to be considered in developing the ranked order. The higher the Numerical Score, the higher the rankings received by the Delphi panel. The challenge was that values were assigned to only the top 15, leaving the balance of the competencies with no value assigned. Using a mean score would not accurately reflect the input from the Delphi panel. This method of using counts and inverted numerical value was used to offset this challenge.

Table 13 shows the top ranked items to be Commitment to Mission and Communication Skills. Both items received nine selections as top 15 competencies with Numerical Scores of 90 and 87, respectively. The panel viewed these two items as being very close to one another in terms of importance.

Table 13: Round Two Results for Top 15 Competencies (Ranked by Selection Count and Numerical Score)

Category	Competency	Count Selections	Numerical Score
Motives	Commitment to Mission/Purpose	9	90
Skills	Communication/Listening	9	87
Traits	Work/Professional Traits	8	50
Skills	Building/Managing a Team	7	80
Knowledge	Board Function & Development	7	62
Skills	Organizational Planning & Development	6	74
Skills	Financial Management & Development	6	54
Motives	Meaningful Work/Seeing Results	6	43
Skills	Leadership Perspective	6	38
Self-concept	Take Responsibility for Development/Success of Organization	6	30
Knowledge	Legal & Operational Requirements	5	50
Knowledge	Information/Learning Skills	5	45
Skills	Problem Solving	5	43
Skills	Respect for People	5	33
Traits	Interpersonal Skills/Traits	5	27
Traits	Team Orientation	5	27
Motives	Personal Values	4	25
Knowledge	Spokesperson & Cheerleader	4	14
Self-concept	Humble	3	34
Self-concept	Outcomes Focus/Results Oriented	3	27
Knowledge	Conflict Resolution & Mediation	3	25
Motives	Enjoyment of Administrative Work	3	18
Skills	Empathy/Compassion	3	18
Skills	Relationships outside the organization	2	18
Skills	Decision Maker	2	14
Self-concept	Self-assured/Confident/Self-aware	2	10
Traits	Patience/Perseverance	2	9
Motives	Compensation	2	2
Traits	Personal Traits	1	14
Motives	Relationships with Colleagues	1	3

A total of 10 competencies were selected by at least six members of the Delphi panel, with the lowest Numerical score in the top ten being 30. Fourteen competencies were selected four times or fewer. This result, coupled with Numerical Scores that trended down in the results, show these competencies to be of less importance.

It is also interesting to note that all five categories are represented in the top 10 ranked competencies, with the skills category having the most with a total of five. There is only one item from the category of Self-concept.

Round Three

The third and final round of this Delphi study provided the panelist with the results from Round Two. They included the mean of the rankings, weighting, and a listing of the order ranked of all 30 items as compiled from the panel's selection of their top 15 in Round Two. A copy of the instructions and results from Round Two sent to the Delphi panel for Round Three is found in Appendix F. The panel members were asked to revise their ranking and weighting from the previous round based on their evaluation of the group responses, which were included. The members of the Delphi panel were invited to change their responses, or to leave them unchanged if they wished. The panel was also asked to evaluate their choices of the Top 15 items in light of the group results from Round Two.

In addition to revising their Top 15 if they wished, panel members were also asked to rank their revised list of Top 15 items on the same 10-100 scaled used for the individual competencies in each category.

Of the nine panelists surveyed in this round, eight returned the material for Round Three.

Ranking by Category

The results from Round Three were compiled and analyzed using the same methodology as in Round Two. The additional element in Round Three was a comparison of the results from each round, with attention given to the changes. Once again, the five categories of competencies were used, and the panelists were asked to review their rankings and weighting in light of the group means and to revise as they saw fit. The mean group rank and weighting, along with the standard deviation for both, can be found in tables 14-18. These tables also include the results from Round Two for comparison purposes.

Table 14 displays the group means and standard deviations for the skill competencies from Round Three. There was some realignment in the ranked order of the competencies from Round Two. Communication/Listening moved from second to first with a mean group ranking of 2.50 in Round Three. This was a higher rank than that achieved in Round Three by Building/Managing a Team (3.00), which dropped to 3.13 in Round Three. The other change in ranking was Leadership Perspective moving to fourth with a group mean rank of 4.25. Overall, the top-ranked competency in the skills category achieved a higher mean group rank and mean group weighting in Round Three, indicating greater importance than in the previous round. Overall, the standard deviation for the mean group ranking was lower in Round Three, indicating less variability, which suggests a higher level of agreement among the panel members concerning the rankings of these competencies.

Table 14: Round Three Results for Skills (Rank and Weight Group Means and Standard Deviation)

	Mean Group Rank	Standard Deviation	Mean Group Weight	Standard Deviation
Communication/Listening	2.50	2.00	82.63	16.41
Building/Managing a Team	3.13	1.55	81.63	16.02
Organizational Planning & Development	4.00	2.78	58.50	30.88
Leadership Perspective	4.25	1.91	62.13	21.71
Financial Management & Development	5.00	1.93	59.25	20.09
Respect for People	5.25	3.11	67.63	18.84
Problem solving	6.63	1.92	60.25	19.71
Decision Maker	6.88	2.17	43.63	20.86
Empathy/Compassion	8.13	1.89	48.63	23.41
Relationships Outside the Organization	9.25	1.49	34.88	28.46

Table 15 presents the Round Three results for the Knowledge category. There was no change in the ranked order from Round Two. The mean group rank for Information and Learning Skills increased from 2.22 to 1.75 in the third round, with a drop in the standard deviation indicating an increase in importance and greater consensus among the panel members regarding the placement of this competency. There were also shifts in the mean group weighting that allowed them to be aligned with the group rankings in terms of importance. The first-ranked item increased its mean group weighting, while the three lowest-ranked items saw a decrease mean group weighting compared with the previous round. These changes from the previous round signal a greater level of agreement among the panel members on the rankings for the knowledge competencies.

Table 15: Round Three Results for Knowledge (Rank and Weight Group Means and Standard Deviation)

	Mean Group Rank	Standard Deviation	Mean Group Weight	Standard Deviation
Information/ Learning Skills	1.75	1.16	75.38	20.45
Board Function & Development	2.50	0.93	68.25	24.00
Legal & Operational Requirements	3.38	1.60	50.25	35.92
Spokesperson/Cheerleader	3.50	1.31	48.88	33.43
Conflict Resolution & Mediation	3.88	1.25	50.50	31.51

The Round Three results for the Traits category of competencies are presented in Table 16. The ranked order of the competencies in this category remained the same as in the previous round. The mean group ranking for Interpersonal Skills increased from 2.00 in the previous round to 1.75 in Round Three. The adjustments in the mean group weighting reinforced the ranked order with an evident increase for the two top-ranked

Table 16: Round Three Results for Traits (Rank and Weight Group Means and Standard Deviation)

	Mean Group Rank	Standard Deviation	Mean Group Weight	Standard Deviation
Interpersonal Skills/Traits	1.75	1.04	85.88	11.36
Work/Professional Traits	2.25	1.16	76.13	22.13
Team Orientation	3.25	0.71	64.50	23.62
Personal Traits	3.88	1.55	44.63	34.22
Patience/Perseverance	3.88	1.36	33.75	22.64

items and a drop in mean group weight for the remaining three items. Some changes in the standard deviation for both mean group rank and weight were evident.

Table 17 presents the results for the motive competencies. This category did not see any changes in the ranked order of the competencies from the previous round. Again, there was evidence of the panel's reaffirming and moving to a greater level of consensus, shown by higher mean scores in ranking and weighting for the top item and a decrease for the last two competencies in the rankings. Standard deviations trended downward as a whole, but were not consistently lower than in the previous round.

Table 17: Round Three Results for Motives (Rank and Weight Groups Means and Standard Deviation)

	Mean Group Rank	Standard Deviation	Mean Group Weight	Standard Deviation
Commitment to Mission/Purpose	1.25	0.46	91.88	11.32
Meaningful Work/Seeing Results	1.88	0.64	81.50	18.59
Relationships w/ Colleagues	3.88	1.13	65.63	27.05
Personal Values	4.13	1.13	54.13	26.10
Enjoyment of Administrative Work	4.75	1.16	33.13	31.05
Compensation	5.13	1.13	39.38	25.83

The Round Three results for Self-concept/Self-understanding are presented in Table 18. This is one of two categories in which the order of the ranked items changed from the previous round. The top two items remained unchanged, but did see slight increases in mean group ranking score and mean group weight, signaling agreement on the placement of the top-ranked competencies in the category. The change in ranking that did occur was the competency of Humility's moving from the fourth to the third position. This change occurred in part because the mean group rank for Humble changed from 3.11 to 3.00, but largely because of the change in rank score for Self-assured fluctuated from 2.89 to 3.13. This is the largest change for any competency in this category. The mean group weight for these items did not correspond to the mean group rank.

Table 18: Round Three Results for Self -concept/Self-understanding (Rank and Weight Groups Means and Standard Deviation)

	Mean Group Rank	Standard Deviation	Mean Group Weight	Standard Deviation
Take Responsibility for Development/Success of Organization	1.63	0.74	82.38	14.87
Outcomes Focus/Results Oriented	2.25	1.04	64.50	30.86
Humble	3.00	1.41	45.63	40.66
Self-assured/Confident/Self-aware	3.13	0.64	57.00	34.51

Top 15 Ranking

In Round Three, the panelists were given the opportunity to revise their selection of their top 15 competencies from the previous round based on the results from other members of the panel. The methodology used to evaluate the results of this ranking was the same as that employed in Round Two. The results are shown in Table 19.

Although there were some changes to the order of the rankings from the previous round, the top eight competencies

189

Table 19: Round Three Results for Top 15 Competencies (Ranked by Selection Count and Numerical Score)

Category	Competency	Count Selections	Numerical Score
Motives	Commitment to Mission/Purpose	8	86
Skills	Communication/Listening	8	96
Traits	Work/Professional Traits	7	51
Skills	Building/Managing a Team	6	74
Knowledge	Board Function & Development	6	55
Skills	Organizational Planning & Development	6	68
Skills	Financial Management & Development	6	55
Motives	Meaningful Work/Seeing Results	6	43
Skills	Problem Solving	6	43
Skills	Leadership Perspective	5	28
Self-concept	Take Responsibility for Development/Success of Organization	5	36
Knowledge	Information/Learning Skills	5	27
Skills	Respect for People	5	31
Skills	Interpersonal Skills/Traits	5	20
Traits	Legal & Operational Requirements	4	36
Traits	Personal Values	4	26
Motives	Spokesperson & Cheerleader	4	5
Knowledge	Outcomes Focus/Results Oriented	4	25
Self-concept	Team Orientation	3	11
Self-concept	Humble	3	34
Knowledge	Self-assured/Confident/Self-aware	3	12
Motives	Conflict Resolution & Mediation	2	11
Skills	Empathy/Compassion	2	15
Skills	Decision Maker	2	3
Skills	Enjoyment of Administrative Work	1	6
Self-concept	Relationships outside the organization	1	12
Traits	Patience/Perseverance	1	9
Motives	Personal Traits	1	14
Traits	Relationships with Colleagues	1	3
Motives	Compensation	0	0

remained the same. The competency of Problem Solving moved into the top ten; Legal & Operational Planning dropped to 15th; and Self-assured moved from the 26th position to the 21st in Round Three. The bottom four competencies remained the same, but with Compensation moving to last place. The stability of

Table 20: Round Three Results for Top 15 Competencies (Ranked by Total Weighting, Mean Weights, and Standard Deviation)

Category	Competency	Sum of Wghtng	Mean Wghtng	Standard Deviation
Motives	Commitment to Mission/Purpose	742	92.75	15.63
Skills	Communication/Listening	586	83.71	14.50
Traits	Work/Professional Traits	462	77.00	19.01
Skills	Building/Managing a Team	443	88.60	9.04
Skills	Organizational Planning & Development	441	88.20	3.83
Skills	Respect for People	381	75.20	14.39
Knowledge	Board Function & Development	353	70.60	34.92
Motives	Meaningful Work/Seeing Results	349	69.00	28.69
Skills	Financial Management & Development	332	66.40	33.87
Skills	Problem Solving	304	60.80	24.86
Self-concept	Take Responsibility for Development/Success of Organization	286	71.50	18.36
Skills	Leadership Perspective	280	70.00	16.51
Knowledge	Information/Learning Skills	279	55.80	9.91
Self-concept	Outcomes Focus/Results Oriented	231	77.00	18.08
Traits	Interpersonal Skills/Traits	215	43.00	28.64
Self-concept	Humble	215	53.75	33.51
Knowledge	Legal & Operational Requirements	209	69.67	26.27
Motives	Personal Values	165	55.00	13.23
Self-concept	Self-assured/Confident/Self-aware	140	46.67	7.64
Knowledge	Conflict Resolution & Mediation	135	67.50	24.75
Knowledge	Spokesperson & Cheerleader	128	32.00	26.32
Skills	Relationships outside the organization	93	93.00	0.00
Skills	Empathy/Compassion	85	42.50	38.89
Traits	Personal Traits	80	80.00	0.00
Traits	Patience/Perseverance	75	37.90	10.61
Traits	Team Orientation	50	25.00	21.21
Motives	Enjoyment of Administrative Work	50	50.00	0.00
Skill	Decision Maker	45	45.00	0.00
Motives	Relationships with Colleagues	10	93.00	0.00
Motives	Compensation	0	0.00	0.00

competencies at both ends of the ranked list suggests the panel was comfortable with their choice of the top 15 competencies in the earlier round. Round Three allowed the Delphi panel members to make adjustments as they desired, but minimal changes resulted in a relatively stable ranking in the third and final round.

The panel was asked to assign weighting on the same 10-100 scale used for the competencies by category. Weighting was assigned only to the 15 items each panel member personally ranked as his or her top 15 competencies. Table 20 shows the total weighting for each item, the mean weight, and the standard deviation of the weight assigned by the Delphi panel.

The most significant element in Table 20 is the Sum of Weighting, which demonstrates the importance of each competency using the weighting assigned by the Delphi panel. The higher the number, the more important that particular competency was in the view of the panel. The weight provides a more precise measurement of the importance of the competencies in relation to one another.

The first five competencies in Table 20 by weighting are identical to those in Table 19, which ranked the competencies by the number of votes received. Commitment to Mission has a summed weighting of 742, and Communication has a summed weighting of 586. The last two competencies in the list are identical with the results in Table 19 as well. Relationship with Colleagues had a summed weighting of 10, while Compensation was not weighted at all because it was not ranked.

One the largest changes is Respect for People's moving from 13th to sixth and Team Orientation's dropping from 19th to 26th position. Overall, while there was some movement in the rankings, changes in ranking based on the two methods were minimal.

Final MAU Analysis

The last step in the analysis of the data is to use the Multi-Attribute Utility (MAU) technique used by Holmes (2005, p. 182) and Clark and Friedman (1982) to further understand the weighting provided by the panelists. The final weighting for each competency within each category was totaled, and then each weighting was divided by the sum of the category. This standardized weight is a representation of the proportion of the total weighted score given across the entire category by each panel member. After the individualized standard weights were calculated, the range, group means, and standard deviation for the weighted scores were determined. This technique was used to compare the difference between weighted values among the panelists while still showing the central tendency of the group.

Tables 21 through 27 present the standardized weight values, standardized weight value ranges, and standard deviation for each item in the five categories from Round Three. The items in each table are listed in ranked order by the mean standardized weighted score, from largest to smallest. A larger group mean standardized weight indicates greater importance, and a smaller score indicates less importance in the opinion of the panel.

Table 21 contains the standardized weight scores for the category of skills. It shows the first two competencies of greatest importance in the skills category by standard weight values to be the same as the top two competencies by ranked order from Round Three. The last three competencies are also the same; however, Empathy/Compassion was rated eighth by standardized weight versus ninth by importance.

Table 21: Standardized Weights for Round Three Skill Competencies

	Minimum	Maximum	Mean	Standard Deviation
Communication/Listening	0.103	0.185	0.140	0.028
Building/Managing a Team	0.104	0.213	0.139	0.033
Respect for People	0.064	0.159	0.114	0.030
Leadership Perspective	0.074	0.151	0.103	0.027
Problem Solving	0.053	0.150	0.101	0.031
Financial Management & Development	0.056	0.138	0.098	0.024
Organizational Planning & Development	0.019	0.144	0.097	0.049
Empathy/Compassion	0.043	0.167	0.081	0.038
Decision Making	0.038	0.106	0.073	0.028
Relationships Outside the Organization	0.019	0.122	0.053	0.039

The most significant difference between the ranking by standard weight in Table 21 and the importance ranking in Table 14 was that Respect for People was ranked sixth by importance, but third based on standardized weighting. Organizational Development fell from the third position in ranked importance to the seventh position when standardized weighting was applied. This change in rankings reflects the relative importance of the items within the categories themselves when considering the distribution of the assigned weighting by the panel. Respect for People was more important to the panel than the ranking by importance revealed.

The results of the standardized weights for the Knowledge competencies are shown in Table 22. These results follow that same ranked order from the importance rankings found in Table 15. The mean score for the highest ranked competencies is 0.267, which is significantly higher than that of the next competency.

Table 22: Standardized Weights for Round Three Knowledge Competencies

	Minimum	Maximum	Mean	Standard Deviation
Information/ Learning Skills	0.154	0.474	0.267	0.098
Board Function & Development	0.105	0.265	0.171	0.052
Legal & Operational Requirements	0.029	0.308	0.167	0.101
Spokesperson/Cheerleader	0.027	0.286	0.167	0.110
Conflict Resolution & Mediation	0.031	0.257	0.167	0.085

This result demonstrated a strong consensus in the panel that this competency was indeed more significant that the other items in this category. Based on the standardized weights, the remaining four competencies were viewed as being very close in importance.

Table 23: Standardized Weights for Round Three Traits Competencies

	Minimum	Maximum	Mean	Standard Deviation
Interpersonal Skills/Traits	0.216	0.323	0.285	0.037
Work/Professional Traits	0.137	0.290	0.246	0.048
Team Orientation	0.039	0.273	0.209	0.072
Personal Traits	0.029	0.353	0.149	0.117
Patience/Perseverance	0.029	0.200	0.111	0.070

Table 23 contains the standardized weights for the Traits category in ranked order. The competency of Interpersonal Skills/Traits had the highest mean standardized weight of 0.285, with Patience scoring the lowest with 0.111. The order here mirrors the ranked order by importance from Table 16. The interval in mean standardized weights was the greatest between Team Orientation and Personal Traits.

The standardized weights results for the Motives category are shown in Table 24. Commitment to Mission had the highest standardized weight at 0.258, followed closely by Meaningful Work at 0.225. The standard deviation for these two items was nearly identical as well. The order of the competencies by standardized weights differed slightly from the importance ranking. Compensation was last when ranked importance was considered, but fifth when ranked by standardized weight, as shown below.

Table 24:Standardized Weights for Round Three Motives Competencies

	Minimum	Maximum	Mean	Standard Deviation
Commitment to Mission/Purpose	0.218	0.304	0.258	0.036
Meaningful Work/Seeing Results	0.179	0.282	0.225	0.037
Relationships w/ Colleagues	0.087	0.254	0.173	0.054
Personal Values	0.022	0.239	0.157	0.079
Compensation	0.025	0.171	0.102	0.054
Enjoyment of Administrative Work	0.024	0.207	0.085	0.066

Table 25 presents the standardized weights for the Self-concept category of competencies. Slight differences exist between the ranking of the competencies by standardized weight and by mean rank order from Round Three. Self-assured ranked third when standardized weight was used, versus a ranking of four by mean rank order. Humility dropped to four in Table 25. The top two ranked items were the same as in Round Two.

Table 25: Standardized Weights for Round Three Self-concept/Self-understanding
Competencies

	Minimum	Maximum	Mean	Standard Deviation
Take Responsibility for Development/Success of Organization	0.245	0.385	0.322	0.049
Outcomes Focus/Results Oriented	0.036	0.340	0.248	0.100
Self-assured/Confident/Self-aware	0.038	0.321	0.212	0.112
Humble	0.025	0.409	0.180	0.160

Chapter Five

Conclusions, Discussions, and Recommendations

The purpose of this study was to develop a competency model for executive leaders of social service organizations in the nonprofit sector. The study also sought to compare these competencies with similar roles in other sectors to see if what, if any, differences could be articulated. The results of these two questions led to the final question of whether a competency model unique to social service organizations could be produced that would be helpful in the recruitment and development of executive leaders in the nonprofit sector.

The study methodology included a Preliminary Survey completed by a convenience sample of leaders in the nonprofit sector to gather general information regarding their personal experience in the nonprofit sector and the current challenges facing their organizations. The Preliminary Survey also provided the opportunity for respondents to indicate interest in participating in the Delphi process, in which the questions regarding the competencies for leaders of social service agencies in the nonprofit sector were developed. This chapter summarizes the conclusions and elucidates the implication of the results for the nonprofit sector. The strengths and weaknesses of the methodology followed are discussed, and suggestions for future research are made.

Conclusions and Discussions

Three conclusions have been drawn from the results of the study. Each of these is presented and then discussed.

Conclusion One

The Delphi panel identified competencies the members viewed as important to effectively lead social service agencies in the nonprofit sector.

The first research question this study sought to address was "What competencies are needed for executives to lead effectively in the social service organization in the nonprofit sector?" The Delphi method was selected as the appropriate method to use in this study. The Delphi method is recognized as being well-suited to complex issues that require a group of experts to share their personal understanding with the goal of arriving at consensus regarding the issue at hand (Adler & Ziglio, 1996; Holmes, 2005; Linstone & Turoff, 2002b; Novakowski & Wellar, 2008; Williams & Webb, 1994). In this study, a panel of 10 individuals with at least five years of experience within social service, nonprofit agencies were asked to consider what they believed to be the most important competencies the leader of a social service agency. Over the course of three rounds they were able to give input, review the group results, and revise their own input based on the group feedback. The goal of the Delphi process is for the panel of experts to arrive at consensus regarding the issue being studied. This consensus could be measured either as a central tendency based on a statistical mean (Hasson, Keeney, & McKenna, 2000, p. 379), or in terms of stability in the answers from one round to the others (Goodman, 1987, p. 373).

One of the unique features of the Delphi method is the provision that panelists can modify or add to previous responses at any point during the study's three rounds of input. The list of competencies that evolved through this process represented a wide range of elements that the panel was able to interact with over the course of the three rounds of the Delphi study. A list of 30 competencies in five different categories was identified by the Delphi panel over the course of this research project. The results were ranked within each category, as well as by overall importance using rank and weight as assigned by the panel.

The group's mean score was the element used to rank each item within its given category. A review of the mean scores and the standard deviation reveal that consensus did develop among the panel members over the course of the study. This conclusion was very evident when a comparison of the top one or two items in each category was done after Round Three. An example of such a comparison can be seen in the Motivation category, where Commitment to Mission had mean group score of 1.25 and a standard deviation of 0.46. This item was followed by Meaningful Work, with a mean group score of 1.88 and a standard deviation of 0.64. The results showed a significant gap between Meaningful

Work and the next item, Relationship with Colleagues, which ended up at 3.88 with a standard deviation of 1.13. This pattern was evident in all the categories.

This pattern, along with the fact that the Skills category saw a change in the top two items from Round Two to Round Three, demonstrated that stability in responses had been achieved, signaling that consensus had been achieved. This stability can also be seen in the consistency of the competencies at the lower end of the rankings. Only the category of Self-concept saw a change, and this was an interchanging of the lower two items between Rounds Two and Three.

The competencies identified were wide ranging in terms of the areas of leadership they represented. The majority of the competencies identified were placed by the researcher into the categories of Skills (10) and Knowledge (5). An additional 15 competencies were identified and placed in the categories of Traits, Motives, and Self-concept/Self-understanding.

The categories themselves were provided by the researcher to ensure that the individual panel members evaluated competency from a broad perspective when they considered the questions in Round One. The intent was to gather the broadest possible range of competencies in Round One and to refine and rank these in subsequent rounds of the study.

One premise of leadership that had been explored in the literature review was that, although leaders certainly need to have certain skills and a body of knowledge, leadership flows from who one is as a person. This means that when leadership competency is viewed in the broadest and most holistic terms, elements of the person of the leader must be taken into consideration as well. Two competency model studies cited earlier in this research, Spencer and Spencer (1993) and Boyatzis (1982), referred to some competencies that related to the person of the leader when competencies such as self-control and self-confidence were mentioned. The panel in this study also cited self-confidence as a competency.

The panel, however, seemed to add other competencies that were not skill or knowledge-based, but that related more closely to the person of the leader. These included elements such as patience, perseverance, empathy, humility, and respect for people. The panel also ranked Commitment to Mission/Purpose as the most important competency for a nonprofit leader of a social service agency. This competency was described as having a passion for the mission of the organization. Passion is not a skill or knowledge; it flows from the values and perspective of the individual. Passion and commitment are rooted in the person of the leader. It is evident from these responses that the Delphi panel did recognize that some aspects of successful leadership in the nonprofit sector flow from the person of the leader, illustrating the principle articulated by Lowney (2003, p. 15) that you lead from who you are as a person. Of the competencies noted above as being tied more closely to the person of the leader, Commitment to Mission was ranked first overall, Respect for People was ranked fifth, Humble was 16th, Empathy was 23rd, and Patience/Perseverance was 26th.

The Delphi panel was also asked in Round Two to assign a ranking of 1-15 to the competencies they deemed most important.

In Round Three, the panel members were given the opportunity to revise their earlier ranking in light of the group results. The panel was also asked to assign a weighting (10-100) to each item they personally ranked. This action resulted in a ranked list of all 30 competencies. All five categories were represented in the top 15 items ranked by the total weight assigned for each item. The most important competency by weight was Commitment to Mission. It also had a low standard deviation, which indicated a high level of agreement among the panel members. Six of the top 15 items were from the Skills category, which could be expected since it was the largest category numerically with 10 competencies.

The breadth within the top 15 competencies was evident not only across the categories, but it also contained two of the competencies noted above as being tied more closely to the person of the leader. These included Commitment to Mission and Respect for People. When looking at the top 15 in this way, the conclusion could be drawn that the Delphi panel presented a balanced view of the competencies required for nonprofit leaders. When all 30 competencies are considered, the picture of leadership competency becomes broader in terms of the competencies areas covered by the model proposed. Overall, the Delphi panel was able to move through the research process and arrive at a model that was well-developed and sufficiently broad in range of competencies covered. The consensus of the panel was evidenced by the stability of responses between rounds two and three, and the lower standard deviation on the top-ranked items in Round Three as compared with Round Two.

Conclusion Two

The competencies required for executive level leaders in the nonprofit sector, while having some similarities to executive roles in other sectors, also have key differences.

The results from the Delphi panel were reviewed in light of the competency models from Spencer and Spencer (1993) and Boyatzis (1982, p. 230). Neither of these models was designed specifically for nonprofit, social sector executive leaders; rather, the models were more generic in nature, but did focus on management. They are, however, both based on extensive research and offer the best comparison for the results of this study. Table 26 shows the comparison of the results from the Delphi study with

Table 26: Comparison of Delphi Study Results and Spencer & Spencer Management Competencies Ordered by Importance

Delphi Study	Spencer & Spencer
Commitment to Mission/Purpose	Impact & Influence
Communication/Listening	Achievement Orientation
Work/Professional Traits	Teamwork & Cooperation
Building/Managing a Team	Analytical Thinking
Organizational Planning & Development	Initiative
Respect for People	Developing Others
Board Function & Development	Self-confidence
Meaningful Work/Seeing Results	Directiveness/Assertiveness
Financial Management & Development	Information Seeking
Problem Solving	Team Leadership
Take Responsibility for Development/Success of organization	Conceptual Thinking
Leadership Perspective	Assumed Competencies:
Information/Learning Skills	Organizational Awareness
Outcomes Focus/Results Oriented	Relationship Building
Interpersonal Skills/Traits	Expertise & Specialized Knowledge
Humble	

a competency model for managers proposed by Spencer and Spencer (1993, p. 201). A comparison of the two models reveals areas of similarities.

Table 26 shows areas of similarity in the models as a whole but is not intended to necessarily show line by line equivalencies throughout the entire table. There are, however, some areas in which the sentiment of the competencies between the two models have similar emphasis. These include competencies such as Commitment to Mission and from this study with the competency of Impact & Influence from Spencer & Spencer. Further similarities exist between Building a Team and Teamwork & Cooperation; Information/Learning Skills and Information Seeking; Meaningful Work/Seeing Results and Achievement Orientation; and finally, Interpersonal Skills/Traits and Relationship Building. These items represent a good degree of similarities between these two models.

There are, however, some key differences between the two models that should be noted. Commitment to the Mission/Purpose and Impact & Influence are similar in that both encompass an aspect of leadership that is personal in nature. Commitment to Mission is the leader focusing on something outside of him or herself, while Impact & Influence has been defined as using one's ability to influence "to get them to support the speaker's agenda" (Spencer & Spencer, 1993, p. 44). The Spencer model displays more concern for the ability of the leader to influence, while the Delphi panel focused less on the leader's ability to influence and more on the object (the organization) or purpose of that influence. The presence of "passion" for organizational purpose was mentioned by more than one member of the Delphi panel in Round One. It may be assumed in the Spencer and Spencer (1993) model that the influence wielded by the leader ought to focus on organizational outcomes, but the Delphi panel chose to plainly articulate this as the single most important competency for a nonprofit leader.

The comparison of the competency list from the Delphi panel and the model from Spencer and Spencer (1993) revealed key differences as well. The most striking difference was the inclusion by the Delphi panel of the competency labeled as Humble. This particular item was ranked 16th by total weight assigned, which suggests a moderate level of importance by the panel; it is unique because there is no equivalent in the Spencer and Spencer model as outlined in Table 26.

The competency Humble was in the category of Self-concept/Self-understanding. The results from Round One contained statements from the panel members highlighting their view of humility as a key competency. The responses included "I believe the effective leader views themselves (*sic*) with humility" and "I am the servant. The more people I hire, the more people I report to." These statements align with the concept of Level 5 leadership articulated by Collins (2001). The Level 5 leader as defined by Collins is "modest and willful, humble and fearless" (p. 22). The Delphi panel captured the humble and modest portion of this perspective. Though the exact words "willful" and "fearless" were not used by the panel in this study, perseverance was mentioned and was defined as the ability to "exercise willpower to stay with it especially when it looks impossible." This statement expresses the second part of Collins' definition of a Level 5 leader as someone who possesses a "ferocious resolve" to get something done (p. 30). This was also illustrated by the competency Outcomes/Results Oriented, which was ranked 14th. When the results from the Delphi panel are evaluated in this way, the alignment with Collins becomes more obvious. The Spencer and Spencer model does not contain these same competencies that allow parallels to be drawn to Collins' Level 5 leadership. Spencer and Spencer (1993) have not included competencies such as humility and the will to succeed. They do include Achievement Orientation, but that was described more in terms of efficiency, effectiveness, goal setting, and cost benefits (Spencer & Spencer, 1993, p. 203). Theirs appears to be a more skill-based approach to outcomes than the perseverance perspective articulated by the Delphi panel.

Another area of competency affirmed by the panel and absent from the Spencer and Spencer (1993) model was Financial Management & Development. Table 26 shows the Spencer and Spencer competency model for mangers, which makes no mention of the financial competency required. Spencer and Spencer do have a Cognitive Cluster of competencies, which contains a competency labeled Technical/Professional/Managerial Expertise (p. 73). The models developed by Spencer and Spencer were not intended to be exhaustive. Some competencies not mentioned are assumed to be mastered and therefore do not need to be mentioned (Spencer & Spencer, 1993, p. 215). It is unknown whether this is the case for Financial Management in the Spencer and Spencer model.

The inclusion in the model from the Delphi panel is indicative of the demand on nonprofit executives to manage the financial affairs of the organization spanning from fundraising, grant writing, budgeting, and reporting. This could be in part because of the economic climate of 2009-2011 that saw a decrease in government funding. The need for competency related to finances could also be in response to the increasing expectations for nonprofits to be well-run, incorporating more management practices used in the corporate sector (Billis, 1993, p. 321; Nanus & Dobbs, 1999, p. 47). The pressure being experienced by nonprofit leaders to have well-developed skills in the area of finances was also evident in the results of Preliminary Survey in this study. The respondents cited funding as being one the greatest challenges being faced, and training in grant writing and budgeting as being an area in which additional training is desired. It is clear from these results that the ability to deal with financial matters was understood by the Delphi panel to be an important component in the success of the nonprofit leader.

Another well-researched competency model was developed by Boyatzis (1982). The work of Spencer and Spencer (1993), as well as of Schroder (1989), has drawn on the research and model of competency proposed by Boyatzis, which developed the idea of "clusters" in competency models but also noted variance in competencies required depending on the level of a given role within an organization. Table 27 contains the listing of top competencies from the Delphi Panel in this study and the competencies from Boyatzis' model for executive-level managers.

The competencies from the Boyatzis model are not presented in
ranked order.

Table 27: Comparison of Delphi Study Results and Boyatzis Competencies

Delphi Study	Boyatzis[1]
Commitment to Mission/Purpose	Concern with impact
Communication/Listening	Diagnostic use of concepts
Work/Professional Traits	Efficiency orientation
Building/Managing a Team	Proactivity
Organizational Planning & Development	Conceptualization
Respect for People	Self-confidence
Board Function & Development	Use of oral presentations
Meaningful Work/Seeing Results	Other Competencies:
Financial Management & Development	Developing others
Problem Solving	Managing group process
Take Responsibility for	Perceptual objectivity
Development/Success of Organization	
Leadership Perspective	
Information/Learning Skills	
Outcomes Focus/Results Oriented	
Interpersonal Skills/Traits	
Humble	

[1] Adapted from *The Competent Manager* by R. E. Boyatzis (1982). John Wiley & Sons.
pp. 226-227.

A careful evaluation of the competencies in Table 27
revealed some areas of similarity. Boyatzis (1982) included a
competency labeled "Concern with Impact." This was described as
the leaders' desire to use their position and influence to bring
about a desired outcome. They are concerned about being viewed
as leaders and influencers and will work to cultivate the image of
being a leader (Boyatzis, 1982, p. 86). This competency is similar
to the Outcomes Focus named by the Delphi panel. Both

competencies underline the desire on the part of the leader to see certain goals achieved. However, the Delphi panel did not, under the guise of this competency, make any suggestions regarding the perspective of the leader related to the position of the leader and the importance that image may have on the ability of the leader to bring about change. The focus of the panel was squarely on concern for outcomes and results.

Some of the elements used by Boyatzis (1982) to describe Concern with Impact are very different from the humility noted by the Delphi panel as being required of a nonprofit leader (p. 86). Concern for position and image is not typically viewed as being compatible with humility. This could be one of the ways in which these two competency models differ from one another.

Another area in which there seemed to be some similarities between the Boyatzis model (1982) and the results of the model from this study had to do with the intellectual side of leadership. Boyatzis noted that a competency leader must have the ability to make use of concepts when evaluating a situation (diagnostic use of concepts). The leader must be able to use what he or she has learned to analyze and understand a situation. The Delphi panel noted that one of the competencies need for leadership was the Information and Learning Skills the leader possessed. The leader must have the ability to learn quickly, know how to acquire the information needed, and always be willing to learn. Although Boyatzis focused on the application and use of the skills the leader already knew and the Delphi panel focused on the ability, skill, and willingness to learn, both models have pointed out the importance of conceptual knowledge in leadership. The difference in focus may be explained in part as resulting from the different timeframes in which these models were developed. Boyatzis did much of his work in the 1970s before publishing in 1982. The knowledge set required and the environment in which organizations operated was more static than those leaders face today. The environment and challenges that leaders face are more complex than before (Martin, 2005, p. 6). Leaders will need to continually grow the knowledge base and develop their skills to remain effective. This is one possible explanation for the different perspective on the Knowledge competency between the two models.

The Delphi panel included Taking Responsibility for Development & Success of the Organization in their list of competencies. This is similar to proactivity noted by Boyatzis (1982), which entailed a disposition toward action that would accomplish the stated goals. Both competencies point toward the requirement that the leader take responsibility for activities that will accomplish organizational goals.

There were a few other areas of similarity. Communication as a competency was evident in both models as well. Boyatzis highlighted Use of Oral Presentations, while the Delphi panel noted a few different aspects of communication with an emphasis on general communication along with the ability to listen. The inclusion of listening does make the Delphi competency slightly different, but it does show two-way communication as being significant for those in leadership today. Similarities are also found with competencies that involved aspects of working with teams. The Delphi panel placed high value on Building and

Managing a Team. Boyatzis noted that Developing Others and Managing Group Process were significant competencies. Although these are not identical, both highlight the importance of the leader's functioning as a facilitator in working with groups in the organizational context.

The final aspect of similarity to highlight in these two models is between Perceptional Objectivity from Boyatzis (1982) and elements of Leadership Perspective from the Delphi panel. Perceptual Objectivity was described by Boyatzis as the ability to see situations from an objective point of view, not allowing one's own subjectivity to adversely affect one's ability to understand a situation. The Delphi panel results included the idea of being able to see the big picture as an element of having a Leadership Perspective. In this respect, both models have acknowledged the importance of the leader's ability to perceive a given situation without allowing personal biases to unduly influence the leader's perception. Self-awareness as described by Lowney (2003), which entails "becoming aware of unhealthy blind spots, or weaknesses that derail them" (p. 27), is a key element in this competency's becoming a reality in the life of the leader. A high level of self-understanding allows leaders to understand when personal biases are present. Leaders do not necessarily need to eliminate all bias; this is likely impossible. The best leaders, however, are aware of their biases and work to account for them in their practice of leadership.

There were also key differences between the Boyatzis model (1982) and the Delphi panel results. One of these was the importance of Commitment to Mission/Purpose. There was no obvious counterpart to this competency in the Boyatzis model. The Boyatzis model also did not include any mention of the Financial Management & Development competency. The inclusion of this factor in the Delphi panel model has been discussed, noting the inherent differences of the funding model employed by the nonprofit sector as being the primary reason for its inclusion. Nonprofit leaders, although not concerned with profit, do need to fund their operations and do so largely through donations, grants, and the sale of services. This difference makes competency in the financial arena, which in this case includes grant writing, imperative. Boyatzis gives no commentary as to the reason for the exclusion of any reference to financial competency in his model.

Conclusion Three
The competencies identified can assist in the recruitment and development of nonprofit leaders needed in the sector.

The literature review has shown a continuing need for individuals to assume executive level leadership roles in the nonprofit sector. Though fewer current nonprofit executives reported that they were planning on leaving their post in the next five years in 2011 (67%) than did in 2006 (75%), the main concern now expressed is how to best prepare new leaders to navigate the transition that will take place (Bell, Moyers, & Wolfred, 2006, p. 5; Bell, Moyers, & Cornelius, 2011. p. 3). The impending turnover that had been predicted in the early 2000s has been delayed, but cannot be delayed forever. Currently, one in six executives in the nonprofit sector are over 60 years of age (Bell, Moyers, & Cornelius, 2011, p. 2). Couple this with Simms' (2009) finding that

22% of senior manager hires in nonprofits were in new roles (p. 4) and the demand for leaders in the nonprofit sector is compounded. The sector faces leadership needs due to retirement and growth.

While the leadership need grows, evidence has been presented suggesting concern regarding the sector's ability to manage this transition. Bell, Moyers, and Cornelius (2011) noted that only 33% of current executives are very confident that their boards will hire the right successor (p. 3). This low confidence stems from a lack of understanding related to the role of executive. Only 18% of executives reported having had an evaluation in the last year that was deemed "very useful" (Bell, Moyers, & Cornelius, 2011. p. 4). This finding illustrates how boards can be lacking a solid understanding regarding the basic function and challenges of leading a nonprofit agency. These are the same boards that, in many cases, are responsible for the hiring of executive-level leaders.

A competency model that has been developed using the Delphi method with a focus on social service agencies within the nonprofit sector can be a useful tool in the hiring process. It would be unwise to assume that the model developed in this study would be a good measure for all nonprofit organizations; however, this model does take into account the unique nature of the sector, showing key competencies for nonprofit leadership. This competency model can provide a tool to help those responsible for hiring to better understand the competencies need for leadership success in today's nonprofit.

A competency model allows for the discussion regarding what it takes to succeed in a given role beyond simple list of skills and takes into consideration motives, traits, knowledge, and self-image, along with skills (Boyatzis, 1982, p. 21; Spencer & Spencer, 1993, p. 13). Boyatzis also noted that effective action takes places when there is an alignment between the individual's abilities or competencies, the requirements of the role, and the organizational environment (Boyatzis, 1982, p. 13). This means that competency models that are developed for a particular type of organization may not be useful in another setting. The interplay among the organizational setting, job demands, and broad-based competencies create the environment in which the success or failure of the leader is measured. This study narrowed itself to consider only social service agencies in the nonprofit sector in an effort to create boundaries regarding the organizational environment and job demands so as to allow the focus to rest on the individual competencies of the leader.

The difference of the model examined in this study has already been contrasted with other researched models proposed by Boyatzis (1982) and Spencer and Spencer (1993). The value of the model for the development and recruitment of nonprofit leaders lies in showing the breadth of competencies highlighted by the Delphi panel. Five categories were presented to the Delphi panel for their input, including Knowledge, Skills, Motives, Traits, and Self-concept/Self-understanding. These categories were chosen to reflect the breadth of competency definitions from Spencer and Spencer and Boyatzis. The panel was asked to rank and weight all the competencies identified in Round One within each category in the second and third rounds. The panel members were free to revise their rankings and weightings from one round to another based on the group results.

The Delphi panel identified Information/Learning Skills as most important in the category of Knowledge. The definition of this competency as articulated by the panel had less to do with the information that a leader possessed and more to do with the capacity of the leader to learn, use available resources to gather information, and be willing to learn. This corresponds with the findings of Schroder and Drucker, who both declared that the skills needed by managers and leaders have changed as society has moved to what has been described as a knowledge society (Drucker, 1994, p. 64; Schroder, 1989, p. 109). The skills needed to lead have shifted from the ability to direct and control to being more fluent and proficient in acquiring and using information. The Delphi panel affirmed this perspective when they ranked Information and Learning Skills higher than any particular knowledge set listed, such as Board Function or Legal Requirements. A leader who is information-literate will possess the ability to identify and fill the knowledge gaps he or she possesses.

In the category of Motives, the Delphi panel ranked Commitment to Mission/Purpose as the item of greatest importance. This position highlights a point of departure from the other competency models reviewed in this study. This particular competency was not found in other models with the same precise focus on the mission of the organization. Not only did this particular competency rank first in the Motive category, but it also was the resounding choice for the most important competency overall. Commitment to Mission had a weight score of 742. The second-ranked item of Communication/Listening had a weight score of 586, followed by Work/Professional Traits at 462. The total weight score allows for a better understanding of the actual interval between the top three competencies not evident by simply reviewing the ranking. The total weight score reveals that Commitment to Mission was viewed by the panel as being first by a margin of 156, while the difference between Communication/Listening and Work/Professional Traits was 124. The intervals drop dramatically after the top three. The weight score and the interval of the scores revealed the panel's consensus on the rank of the competencies chosen. Commitment to Mission was clearly the most important competency when evaluating the results from the Delphi panel.

Commitment to Mission was unique in that one would not typically think of it as being a competency. The models have shown that competency for leadership includes more than skill and knowledge. It also includes traits and motives related quite closely to the person of the leader. Some aspects of successful leadership are deeply rooted in the values and person of the leader. This is an example of a competency that fits that description.

One lens through which to view the pre-eminence placed on the purpose of the organization can be viewed as an outworking of servant-leadership. Servant-leadership seeks the good of those being led, or, in the words of Greenleaf, "to make sure that other people's highest priority needs are being served" (Greenleaf, 1995,

p. 22). The importance of organizational purpose or commitment to the mission, when it is understood that social service agencies exist solely for the purpose of serving, should not be a surprise. Though the term *servant-leadership* was not used by the panel members, the sentiment was evident in Commitment to Mission's being chosen first among the rest of the competencies. It was also expressed by one panel member when the individual wrote, "I am the servant. The more people I hire, the more people I report to."

In the category of Self-concept/Self-understanding, the Delphi panel ranked Taking Responsibility for Development/ Success of Organization as being their choice for the most important competency. The ideas submitted by the panel for this particular competency emphasized the importance of the leader's assuming the roles of primary decision maker, visionary, and caretaker regarding the organization's health. Typically when one thinks of self-concept or self-understanding, the idea of self-awareness is included. The Delphi panel made this connection as well, but ranked competency encompassing the idea of self-awareness as last in this category. The literature review has shown how self-awareness has a place in leadership competency models (Boyatzis, 1982, p. 26) as well as in general leadership thought as practiced by the Jesuit order (Lowney, 2003, p. 15).

The panel gave little feedback as to why the particular order was established, with the competency of Assuming Responsibility ranking ahead of other competencies such as Outcomes Focus, Humble, and Self-awareness. It is important to point out that all of these competencies were considered important enough to be included, but the order was not necessarily expected in light of the literature review. An example of this can be seen in the emphasis on the trait of humility in senior leadership articulated by Collins (2005) when discussing a Level Five leader. One possible explanation has been offered by Spencer and Spencer (1993) when they note that some competencies are assumed to be mastered and present by one who reaches upper levels in the organization. This may be the case with the competencies in this category. It is assumed that the leaders have sufficiently mastered all these competencies, but in the case of nonprofit organizations, a sense of ownership for the success of the organization was of particular importance. This principle was noted by Spencer and Spencer in 1993 when evaluating the difference in competencies found from one level of leadership to another (Spencer & Spencer, 1993, p. 215).

The Skill category contained the most competencies (10) as selected by the Delphi panel. This reveals a perspective that while there are other competencies required for nonprofit leaders, what a leader is capable of doing is critical. The underlying or latent competencies undergird the action but the Skill competencies are the most easily identified and articulated. The Skill competencies covered a broad range of expectations for executive leaders. Overall, the competencies found in all categories had a natural and logical fit with their given category. The one competency found in the Skills category that seemingly could have been placed in another category was Empathy/Compassion. This competency could have been placed under Traits or Motives. Empathy/Compassion was left in the Skills category because it was placed here by the panel. This placement would emphasize the value of a visible outworking of the leaders' concern for people and the organization portrayed by the action taken by the leader.

Placement in another category such as Motive or Trait could diminish this feature of Empathy/Compassion, placing more emphasis on the underlying values of the individual rather than on the tangible evidence of the compassion as seen in the actions of the leader. This idea highlights another important feature of the competency model Boyatzis (1982) highlighted in his work. All competencies demonstrated in the life of an individual are rooted in the motives and traits upon which the individual builds self-image and social roles, which in turn feed skills that lead to actions (p. 34). This study did not attempt to define the relationship between skills and the motives or traits that may support them.

The Delphi panel chose to rank Communication/Listening as the most important competency in the Skills category. When evaluating the rankings based on the weight group mean scores, the interval between Communication and the next competency, Building/Managing a Team, was very small (82.63 versus 81.63). These two competencies were identified as being the most important and were set apart from the rest of the list by the Delphi panel. The emphasis on communication and working with a team of people from the panel fits well with the nonprofit leadership model presented by Nanus and Dobbs (1999). The authors highlighted six roles critical for the nonprofit leader, including visionary, strategist, politician, campaigner, coach, and change agent (pp. 17-19). A common thread noted in the description of these roles was the element of communication. Success in these roles requires good communication skills, a necessity noted by the Delphi panel as well.

The panel also recognized the importance of the leader's building and leading a team of people who will contribute to mission accomplishment. The increasing importance of teams in the successful operation of nonprofits would be in keeping with the trend in business toward using teams (Barrett & Beeson, 2002, p. 12). Teamwork was also noted in the Spencer competency model (Spencer & Spencer, 1993, p. 204). Another factor contributing the importance of teams could be the professionalization occurring in the nonprofit sector (Nanus & Dobbs, 1999, p. 47; Salamon, 2002, pp. 38-39). The skill set required to meet the requirements of this professionalization is difficult to find in a single individual, necessitating a team approach to leadership in today's nonprofits. These are all factors contributing to the choice by the panel to have Building/Managing a Team ranked highly as a skill for a nonprofit leader. The presence, or the necessity of developing, this competency in a nonprofit leader is clear when all these factors are considered.

The Delphi panel placed Interpersonal Skills/Traits first in the Traits category. The competency entailed the idea of social intelligence, which encompasses the way in which an individual interacts with and relates to others. The executive is responsible for interacting with a wide variety of stakeholders. This effort requires the ability to be friendly, outgoing, and in possession of the ability to understand circumstances from the perspective of other individuals. The absence or limited nature of this competency in the person of the leader would hamper his or her efforts to lead effectively because of the variety of stakeholders with whom the executive needs to interact. The stakeholders would include those inside as well as outside the organization, those who support the nonprofit as well as those served by the nonprofit (Nanus & Dobbs, 1999, p. 18). The presence or strength in the leader of this particular competency would be crucial in assessing the leader's potential for success.

It has been established that the ability to accomplish organizational purpose can be enhanced when individual competence is recognized and nurtured (Doyle, 1995, p. 29). This study has provided a listing of competencies that can serve as a baseline for doing such assessments. This list can be helpful not only when conducting further training, but also in the hiring process. One of the helpful features of the results was the ranked list of all 30 competencies based on the group weight provided in Round Three. This ranking corresponded closely to the ranking based on the number of times competencies were ranked on the top 15 by the panel members. The top 15 competencies by group weight score included competencies from each of the five categories, including at least the top two from each category.

The one result that did not follow the expected pattern was that Work/Professional Traits, which was second in the Traits category, was third overall, while Interpersonal Skills, which has already been discussed, was 15th. The former competency has a strong focus on performance- or work-related aspects of leadership, such as being a role model, flexibility, dependability, and delegation, as opposed to the "soft" skills of leadership. This anomaly in the results would need to be investigated further to offer a greater understanding of the reasons for this particular result.

The absence or very weak presence of any of the top 15 items from this study would be a signal for those seeking to fill a position that a greater level of consideration should be given to the match of the candidate to the position. It is possible that the particular organization does not need the candidate to have mastered a particular competency if that competency is not needed or there is another way to meet this need. An example may be that of the competency of Organizational Planning & Development. The executive leader may not need to possess the competency if someone else in the organization, a staff or board member, has the skills and is willing to fill this void. However, if this strategy is to work, all parties must understand that the deficiency exists and be in agreement regarding how this deficiency will be met.

This perspective on competency was discussed by Prahaland and Hamel (1990) when they wrote of organizational competency. Organizational competency was defined as the collection of learning found in an organization pertinent to the outcomes desired (p. 82). Certain competencies are required for any organization to achieve its purpose. They must exist within the organization or be at the disposal of the organization.

This study has provided a listing of competencies for boards and other leadership teams to consider when assessing the organizational competencies required. Having this type of competency list allows this assessment to take place and for plans to be implemented that allow the organization the best chance of success. Based on the overall staffing of the organization, the participation of the board, the current organizational posture, and future plans, the order of or the competencies themselves may vary somewhat (Bergenhenegouwen, Horn, & Mooijman, 1996, p. 30). However, Commitment to Mission/Purpose would likely remain the most important competency desired of an executive leader. This one would be foundational to all other competencies.

Le Deist and Winter (2005) have discussed two approaches in the use of competency models. The first was to evaluate a given role and create a list of competencies required for success in that role. This study sought to define such a list for social service agencies in the nonprofit sector. The results give those seeking to hire executive leaders a measure by which to assess potential candidates. This approach allows for a matching of individual competencies with the demands of the role.

The second approach to the use of competency as noted by Le Deist and Winter (2005) was for human resource development. This approach was not to develop competencies for a particular role or organization, but rather to develop competencies that would be transferable to a variety of organizations (p. 28). The results of this study would also be used to do just this: develop senior leaders for a variety of social service organizations in the nonprofit sector. Both approaches are valid uses of competency models.

There were two outcomes of this study that I found very interesting. The first was that the panel identified many competencies found in other models. This speaks to the reliability of this study when compared with the outcomes of other well-researched competency models. It also shows there appear to be competencies that are common across all types of organizations though the importance and emphasis of the individual competencies will vary.

The other outcome of most interest to me was the prominence given to Commitment to Mission/Purpose by all panel members. This competency was strongly supported by all panel members throughout all three rounds of the study. Commitment to Mission is a competency that is unique from other competency models used for comparison purposes. In light of the challenges faced by nonprofit leaders, their commitment to the organization's mission is critical for success. The placement of a competency which flows from the personal values of the leader demonstrates that for leaders in the nonprofit sector, leading is inexplicitly tied to the person of the leader.

This would suggest that leading on the nonprofit sector requires more than just the right skill set but also that the leader's values and personal mission must align with the organization which they lead. This competency must not be overlooked in the recruiting or development of nonprofit leaders.

The aspect of the competency that this study did not address is whether this competency can be developed or, because it is driven by personal values, is discovered.

This is an important distinction that would be beneficial to better understand in the process of utilizing these competencies in the nonprofit sector.

Limitations of the Study

A Preliminary Survey was used in this study to accomplish two ends: first, to gain a better understanding of the current status of nonprofit organizations affiliated with the Nonprofit Association of Oregon; and second, to populate the Delphi panel for the competency research portion of this study. With only 22 responses to the Preliminary Survey, it is not possible to view the results as being representative of the nonprofit sector in a way that would allow generalizations to be made to a larger population. The Preliminary Survey was a greater success in gathering panel members for the Delphi portion of the study. Six of the 10 panel members were selected from a group of 10 who indicated interest in the Delphi panel. The remaining four panel members were recruited using contacts known to me. This method of selecting the Delphi panel could have introduced a measure of self-selection into the process. Using a version of the snowball technique to select part of the Delphi panel could have also limited the breadth of experience and perspectives regarding the competencies for nonprofit leaders. However, this eventuality may have been mitigated somewhat by ensuring that the panel included not only executive directors of social service, nonprofit agencies, but also board members, educators, and volunteers.

Another limitation of the study can be seen in a methodological decision to focus the data gathering and evaluation on the data provided by the panel, with minimal attention given to the reasons that panel members chose their rankings or weighting measures. Asking the panel to provide written rationale for their responses could possibly have provided greater clarity on the rankings and weighting, which in turn might have altered the final results. Boyatzis (1982), in his work on competency models, viewed the evaluation of thought processes behind the chosen competencies as a valuable aspect of building a valid and reliable competency model (p. 57). Since this process would demand too much of the Delphi panel and require unavailable resources, this aspect of the research was not fully developed. However, the Delphi panel was given opportunity to comment on any aspects of the material sent to them in all three rounds of the study.

The study had other limitations that potentially affected the validity and applicability of the results. These include:

1. All panel members were located in Oregon. Some of the organizations represented served clientele outside the region, but all organizations were based in Oregon.

2. The Delphi panel began with 10 participants in Round One. One panel member was lost in each round. The results in Round Three were based on responses from eight panelists, which may have decreased the validity and reliability of the results.

3. Caution must be used in applying the results of this study to the nonprofit sector as a whole. This study focused on a specific group within the nonprofit sector.

4. The study does not address how to measure or assess the presence of these competencies in current or aspiring nonprofit leaders.

Recommendations for Further Study

This was a preliminary and an exploratory study on the competencies required for a leader of a social service, nonprofit organization. The study was intentionally focused so as to develop a competency model for this particular type of nonprofit leader. The study also sought to evaluate the results against models developed for other sectors. The study was able to accomplish both of these outcomes. However, certain areas of competency for nonprofit leaders warrant further research. These include the following areas.

1. Assess the applicability of this model with other types of nonprofit organizations by doing targeted surveys with executive directors, board members, and other stakeholders.

2. Develop or revise a current valid and reliable method of assessing competencies that could be used with current and aspiring nonprofit leaders.

3. Evaluate current training and education programs that target nonprofit leaders to assess which of the competencies from this model are addressed.

4. Replicate this study with a second Delphi panel of experts to provide additional data important to this topic.

5. Continue monitoring leadership needs in the nonprofit sector and assess whether the plans in place or being made address the evolving needs.

6. Use the model in this study to inform the development of training programs for executive-level leaders in nonprofit organizations.

The model developed in this study must be viewed as a "point in time" tool in what ought to be an ongoing discussion regarding the competencies required to lead in the nonprofit sector. Although is it is difficult to predict the "shelf life" of this model, in the face of evolving needs and challenges, it is unrealistic to view this or any other model as static.

Continued study and dialogue are two methods that can be used to ensure the current understanding of leadership competencies for nonprofits is being used.

This study has provided a starting point for continued study and reflection on the leadership competencies needed for an effective nonprofit sector, which is vital to our contemporary society (Spencer & Spencer, 1993).

References

The state of nonprofit America (2002). Washington D.C.: Brookings Institution Press.

Abbott, S. (2009). Social capital and health: The problematic roles of social networks and social surveys. *Health Sociology Review, 18*(3), 297-306.

Adler, M. & Ziglio, E. (1996). *Gazing into the oracle: The Delphi method and its application to social policy and public health.* London, Great Britain: Jessica Kingsley.

Babbie, E. (2004). *The practice of social research.* Belmont, CA: Thomson Wadsworth.

Barner, R. (2000). Five steps to leadership competencies. (Cover story). *Training & Development, 54*(3), 47-51.

Barrett, A. & Beeson, J. (2002). *Developing business leaders for 2010.* New York, NY.The Conference Board

Barrett, G. V. & Depinet, R. L. (1991). A reconsideration of testing for competence rather than for intelligence. *American Psychologist, 46*(10), 1012.

Bell, J., Moyers, R., & Cornelius, M. (2011). *Daring to lead 2011.*Compass Point. Retrieved from http://daringtolead.org/

Bell, J., Moyers, R., & Wolfred, T. (2006). *Daring to Lead 2006.*Compass Point. Retrieved from http://www.compass point.org/assets/194_daringtolead06final.pdf

Bergenhenegouwen, G. J., Horn, H. F. K., & Mooijman, E. A. M. (1996). Competence development - a challenge for HRM professionals: Core competences of organizations as guidelines for the development of employees. *Journal of European Industrial Training, 20*(9), 29-35.

Bielefeld, W. (2006). Quantitative research for nonprofit management. *Nonprofit Management & Leadership, 16*(4), 395-409.

Billis, D. (1993). What can nonprofits and businesses learn from each other? In D.C. Hammack & D.R. Young (Eds.), *Nonprofit organizations in a market economy* (pp. 319-341). San Francisco, CA: Jossey-Bass.

Block, S. R. (2001). A history of the discipline. In S.J. Ott (Ed.), *The nature of the nonprofit sector* (pp. 97-111). Boulder, CO: Westview Press.

Boon, J. & van der Klink, M. (2002). Competencies: The triumph of a fuzzy concept. *Proceedings of the Academy of Human Resource Development, Honolulu, HA,* 350-357.

Boris, E. T. & Steuerle, C. E. (2006). Scope and dimensions of the nonprofit sector. In W.W. Powell & R.J. Steinberg (Eds.), *The non-profit sector: A research handbook* (pp. 66-88). New Haven, CT: Yale University Press.

Bowman, S. (2003). What corporates can learn from not-for-profit strategy-setting. *Mt Eliza Business Review, 6*(1), 56-61.

Boyatzis, R. E. (1982). *The competent manager: A model for effective performance.* New York, NY: John Wiley & Sons.

Boyatzis, R. E. (1983). *The competent manager: A model for effective performance.* New York: John Wiley & Sons.

Brown, S. K. (2009). *A year-end look at the economic slowdown's impact on middle-aged and older Americans.* Washington D.C.AARP. Retrieved from http://assets.aarp.org/rgcenter/econ/economic_slowdown_09.pdf

Brownell, J. & Goldsmith, M. (2006). Meeting the competency needs of global leaders: A partnership approach. *Human resource management, 45*(3), 309-336.

Bryne, J. A. (1990, March 26). Profiting from the nonprofits. *Business Week, 3151,* 66

Bryson, J. M., Ackermann, F., & Eden, C. (2007). Putting the resource-based view of strategy and distinctive competencies to work in public organizations. *Public Administration Review, 67*(4), 702-717.

Cabrera, E. F. & Raju, N. S. (2001). Utility analysis: Current trends and future directions. *International Journal of Selection & Assessment, 9*(1/2), 92.

Cameron, H. (2004). The nonprofit phenomenon: Internet resources for nonprofit organizations. Retrieved from http://www.infotoday.com/searcher/feb04/cameron.shtml

Carbone, R. F. (1993). Marketplace practices and fundraising ethics. In D.C. Hammack & D.R. Young (Eds.), *Nonprofit organizations in a market economy* (pp. 294-315). San Francisco, CA: Jossey-Bass.

Cheetham, G. & Chivers, G. (1996). Towards a holistic model of professional competence. *Journal of European Industrial Training, 20*(5), 20-30.

Cheetham, G. & Chivers, G. (1998). The reflective (and competent) practitioner: A model of professional competence which seeks to harmonise the reflective practitioner and competence-based approaches. *Journal of European Industrial Training,* *22*(6/7), 267.

Clark, A. & Friedman, M. J. (1982). The relative importance of treatment outcomes: A Delphi group weighting in mental health. *Evaluation Review,* *6*(1), 79-93.

Cockerill, T., Hunt, J., & Schroder, H. (1995). Managerial competencies: Fact or fiction? *Business Strategy Review,* *6*(3), 1.

Collins, J. (2001). *Good to great.* New York, NY: Harper Business.

Collins, J. (2005). Level 5 leadership: The triumph of humility and fierce resolve. *Harvard Business Review,* *83*(7/8), 136-146.

Colteryahn, K. & Davis, P. (2004). Trends you need to know. *T+D,* *58*(1), 28-36.

Conger, J. A. & Ready, D. A. (2004). Rethinking leadership competencies. *Leader to Leader,* *2004*(32), 41-47.

Creswell, J. W. (1994). *Research design.* Thousand Oaks, CA: Sage.

Critcher, C. & Gladstone, B. (1998). Utilizing the Delphi technique in policy discussion: A case study of a privatized utility in Britain. *Public Administration,* *76*(3), 431-449.

Dainty, A. R. J., Cheng, M., & Moore, D. R. (2005). Competency-based model for predicting construction project managers performance. *Journal of Management in Engineering,* *21*(1), 2-9.

Dalkey, N. & Helmer, O. (1963). An experimental application of the Delphi method to the use of experts. *Management Science, 9*(3), 458-467.

Dalkey, N. C. (1968). *Experiments in group prediction.* Santa Monica, CA: RAND.

Davis, P., Naughton, J., & Rothwell, W. (2004). New roles and new competencies for the professional. *T+D, 58*(4), 26-36.

Development Resource Group Inc. (2008). 2006 nonprofit CEO survey results. Retrieved from http://www.drgnyc.com/ 2006_Survey/Index.htm

Doyle, P. (1995). Marketing in the new millennium. *European Journal of Marketing, 29*(13), 23-41.

Drucker, P. F. (1998). Management's new paradigms. (Cover story). *Forbes, 162*(7), 152-177.

Drucker, P. F. (1989). What business can learn from nonprofits. *Harvard Business Review, 67*(4), 88.

Drucker, P. F. (1990). *Managing the non-profit organization.* New York, NY: HarperBusiness.

Drucker, P. F. (1994). The age of social transformation. *Atlantic Monthly, 274*(5), 53-80.

Drucker, P. F. (1996). Not enough generals were killed. In F. Hesselbein, M. Goldsmith, & R. Beckhard (Eds.), *The leader of the future* (pp. xi-xv). San Francisco, CA: Jossey-Bass.

Dubois, D. D. & Rothwell, W. (2004). *Competency-based human resource management.* Palo Alto, CA: Davies-Black Publishing.

Edmunds, H. (1999). *The focus group research handbook.* Chicago, IL: NTC Business Books.

Eisenberg, P. (2004). Solving the nonprofit leadership crisis will take much work. *Chronicle of Philanthropy, 17*(5), 44-45.

Elkin, G. (1990). Competency-based human resource development. *Industrial & Commercial Training, 22*(4), 20.

Fallows, J. (1985). The case against credentialism. *Atlantic, 256*(6), 49.

Flanagan, J. C. (1954). The critical incident technique. *Psychological Bulletin, 51*327-358.

Fleishman, J. L. (2007). *The foundation: A great American secret.* New York, NY: Public Affairs.

Frumkin, P. (2002). *On being nonprofit.* Cambridge, MA: Harvard University Press.

Fulmer, R. M. & Wagner, S. (1999). Leadership: Lessons from the best. *Training & Development, 53*(3), 28-32.

Gelatt, J. P. (1992). *Managing nonprofit organizations in the 21st century.* Phoenix, AZ: Oryx Press.

Gibson, L. J. & Miller, M. M. (1990). A Delphi model for planning 'preemptive' regional economic diversification. *Economic Development Review, 8*(2), 34.

Gliddon, D. G. (2006). Forecasting a competency model for innovation leaders using a modified Delphi technique. *Dissertation Abstracts International, 51,* 5222.

Goldschmidt, P. G. (1975). Scientific inquiry or political critique? Remarks on Delphi assessment, expert opinion, forecasting, and group process by H. Sackman. *Technological Forecasting and Social Change, 7*(2), 195-213.

Goodman, C. M. (1987). The Delphi technique: A critique. *Journal of Advanced Nursing, 12*(6), 729-734.

Greenleaf, R. (1995). Servant leadership. In J.T. Wren (Ed.), *The leader's companion* (pp. 18-23). New York, NY: The Free Press.

Hailey, J. & James, R. (2004). Trees die from the top: International perspectives on NGO leadership development. *Voluntas, 15*(4), 343-353.

Haines, S. G. (1999). *Understanding systems thinking & learning.* Amherst, MA: HRD Press.

Hall, P. D. (2006). A historical overview of philanthropy, voluntary associations, and nonprofit organizations in the United States, 1600-2000. In W.W. Powell & R.J. Steinberg (Eds.), *The non-profit sector: A research handbook* (pp. 32-65). New Haven, CT: Yale University Press.

Hammack, D. C. & Young, D. R. (1993). Perspectives on nonprofits in the marketplace. In D.C. Hammack & D.R. Young (Eds.), *Nonprofit organizations in a market economy-* San Francisco, CA: Jossey-Bass.

Hansen, L. S. & Reynolds, C. J. (2010). The future of industrial technology education at the K-12 level. Retrieved from http://scholar.lib.vt.edu/ejournals/JITE/v4on4/hansen.html

Hargrove, R. (1995). *Masterful coaching.* San Francisco, CA: Jossey-Bass.

Hasson, F., Keeney, S., & McKenna, H. (2000). Research guidelines for the Delphi survey technique. *Journal of Advanced Nursing, 32*1008-1015.

Hayes, T. (2007). Delphi study of the future of marketing of higher education. *Journal of Business Research, 60*(9), 927-931.

Helman, R., Copeland, C., & VanDerhei, J. (2009). *The 2009 retirement confidence survey: Economy drives confidence to record lows; many looking to work longer.* Washington D.C.Employee Benefit Research Institute. Retrieved from http://www.ebri.org/pdf/briefspdf/EBRI_IB_4-2009_RCS2.pdf

Hodkinson, P. & Issit, M. (1995). Competence, professionalism and vocational education and training. In P. Hodkinson & M. Issit (Eds.), *The challenge of competence* (pp. 146-156). New York, NY: Cassell.

Holmes, W. M. (2005). Emerging practice in occupational therapy: An exploratory study of its nature and competencies for practice. *Dissertation Abstracts International,* 66, 11B. UMI No. 3195778,

Kaye, B. L. (2005). *Love 'em or lose 'em : Getting good people to stay.* San Francisco, CA: Berrett-Koehler.

Keeney, S., Hasson, F., & McKenna, H. (2006). Consulting the oracle: Ten lessons from using the Delphi technique in nursing research. *Journal of Advanced Nursing, 53*(2), 205-212.

Klemp, G. O. (2001). Competence in context. In J. Raven & J. Stephenson (Eds.), *Competence in the learning society* (pp. 129-147). New York: Peter Lang.

Korngold, A. (2006). Developing visionary leaders. *Leader to Leader, 40*(Spring 2006), 45-50.

Krejci, J. W. & Malin, S. (1997). Impact of leadership development of competencies. *Nursing Economic$, 15*(5), 235-241.

Lagoudis, I. N., Lalwani, C. S., & Naim, M. M. (2006). Ranking of factors contributing to higher performance in the ocean

238

transportation industry: a multi-attribute utility theory approach. *Maritime Policy & Management, 33*(4), 345-369.

Larreche, J. C. & Montgomery, D. B. (1977). A framework for the comparison of marketing models: A Delphi study. *Journal of Marketing Research, 14*(4), 487-498.

Le Deist, F. D. & Winterton, J. (2005). What is competence? *Human Resource Development International, 8*(1), 27-46.

Linstone, H. E. (2002). Eight basic pitfalls: A checklist. In H.E. Linstone & M. Turoff (Eds.), *The delphi method: Techniques and applications* (pp. 559-571). Portland, OR:

Linstone, H. E. & Turoff, M. (2002b). *The Delphi method: Techniques and applications.* Retreived from http://is.njit. edu/pubs/delphibook/

Linstone, H. E. & Turoff, M. (2002a). Introduction. In H.E. Linstone & M. Turoff (Eds.), *The delphi method: Techniques and applications* (pp. 3-12). Portland, OR:

Lowney, C. (2003). *Heroic leadership: Best practices from a 450-year-old company that changed the world.* Chicago, IL: Loyola Press.

Mansfield, B. (1993). Competence-based qualifications: A response. *Journal of European Industrial Training, 17*(3), 19-22.

Mansfield, B. (2004). Competence in transition. *Journal of European Industrial Training, 28*(2-4), 296-309.

Martin, A. (2005). *The changing nature of leadership.*The Center for Creative Leadership. Retrieved from http://www.ccl.org/ leadership/pdf/research/NatureLeadership.pdf

Martino, J. P. (1983). *Technological forecasting for decision making*. New York, NY: North-Hollan.

McClelland, D. C. (1973). Testing for competence rather than for "intelligence". *American Psychologist, 28*(1), 1-14.

McClelland, D. C. (1998). Identifying competencies with behavioral-event interviews. *Psychological Science, 9*(5), 331.

McClelland, D. C. (1993). Intelligence is not the best predictor of job performance. *Current Directions in Psychological Science, 2*(1), 5-6.

Mintzbcrg, H. (1975). The manager's job: Folklore and fact. *Harvard Business Review, 4 (July-August 1975)*(53), 49-53.

Mussi, S. (1999). Facilitating the use of multi-attribute utility theory in expert systems: An aid for identifying the right relative importance weights of attributes. *Expert Systems, 16*(2), 87.

Nanus, B. & Dobbs, S. M. (1999). *Leaders who make a difference*. San Francisco, CA: Jossey-Bass.

Norris, N. (1991). The trouble with competence. *Cambridge Journal of Education, 21*(3), 331-341.

Novakowski, N. & Wellar, B. (2008). Using the Delphi technique in normative planning research: Methodological design considerations. *Environment and Planning, 40*1485-1500.

Okhuysen, G. A. & Eisenhardt, K. M. (2002). Integrating knowledge in groups: How formal interventions enable flexibility. *Organization Science, 13*(4), 370-386.

Olshfski, D. & Joseph, A. (1991). Assessing training needs of executives using the Delphi technique. *Public Productivity & Management Review, 14*(3), 297-301.

Patton, M. Q. (2002). *Qualitative research & evaluation methods*. Thousand Oaks, CA: Sage.

Peterson, T. & Van Fleet , D. D. (2008). A tale of two situations: An empirical study of behavior by not-for-profit managerial leaders. *Public Performance & Management Review, 31*(4), 503-516.

Plas, J. M. & Lewis, S. E. (2001). *Person-centered leadership for nonprofit organizations*. Thousand Oaks, CA: Sage.

Porras, J. C. & Collins, J. (1994). *Built to last: Successful habits of visionary companies*. New York: Harper Business.

Powell, C. (2003). The Delphi technique: Myths and realities. *Journal of Advanced Nursing, 41*(4), 376-382.

Prahalad, C. K. & Hamel, G. (1990). The core competence of the corporation. *Harvard Business Review, 68*(3), 79-91.

Project Team (2005). *Towards a human resource council for the voluntary/non-profit sector*. Ottawa, Canada.Human Resource Sector Council.

Raven, J. (2001a). Issues raised by the studies of competence. In J. Raven & J. Stephenson (Eds.), *Competence in the learning society* (pp. 163-177). New York, NY: Peter Lang.

Raven, J. (2001b). The McBer competency framework. In J. Raven & J. Stephenson (Eds.), *Competence in the learning society* (pp. 121-127). New York, NY: Peter Lang.

Ree, M. J. & Earles, J. A. (1992). Intelligence is the best predictor of job performance. *Current Directions in Psychological Science, 1*(3), 86-89.

Robbins, K. C. (2006). The nonprofit sector in historical perspective: Traditions of philanthropy in the west. In W.W.

Powell & R.J. Steinberg (Eds.), *The non-profit sector: A research handbook* (pp. 13-31). New Haven, CT: Yale University Press.

Robertson, I. & Gibbons, P. (1999). Understanding management performance. *British Journal of Management, 10*(1), 5-12.

Rothwell, W. & Wellins, R. (2004). Mapping your future: Putting new competencies to work for you. *T+D, 58*(5), 1-8.

Rotondi, A. & Gustafson, D. (1996). Theoretical, methodological, and practical issues arising out of the Delphi method. In M. Adler & E. Ziglio (Eds.), *Gazing into the oracle: The delphi method and its application to social policy and public health* (pp. 34-55). London, UK: Jessica Kingsley Publishers.

Rowley, K. M. (2007). Critical characteristics of future community college presidents: A delphi study. (Doctoral dissertation, University of La Verne, 2007). *Dissertation Abstracts International, 68,* 4587.

Ruth, D. (2006). Frameworks of managerial competence: limits, problems and suggestions. *Journal of European Industrial Training, 30*(3), 206-226.

Sackman, H. (1975). *Delphi critique: Expert opinion, forecasting, and group process.* Boston, MA: Lexington Books.

Salamon, L. M. (2003). *The resilient sector: The state of nonprofit America.* Washington D.C.: Brookings Institute Press.

Salamon, L. M. (2001). Scope and structure: The anatomy of America's nonprofit sector. In S.J. Ott (Ed.), *The nature of the nonprofit sector-* Boulder, CO: Westview Press.

Salamon, L. M. (2002). The resilient sector: The state of nonprofit America. In L.M. Salamon (Ed.), *The state of nonprofit*

America (pp. 3-61). Washington D.C.: Brookings Institution Press.

Schroder, H. M. (1989). *Managerial competence*. Dubuque, IA: Kendall/Hunt Publishing Company.

Seel, K. E. (2006). Boundary spanning: A grounded theory of sustainability in Canada's nonprofit sector. (University of Calgary).Unpublished doctoral dissertation, Calgary. Alberta, Canada.

Simms, D. (2009). *Finding leaders for Amercia's nonprofits*. San Francisco.Bridgespan Group

Skogen, K. & Thrane, C. (2008). Wolves in context: Using survey data to situate attitudes within a wider cultural framework. *Society & Natural Resources, 21*(1), 17-33.

Smith, J. P. (2000). Nonprofit management education in the United States. *Vital Speeches of the Day, 66*(6), 182.

Smith, S. R. (2002). Social services. In L.M. Salamon (Ed.), *The state of nonprofit America* (pp. 149-186). Washington D.C.: Brookings Institution Press.

Soosay, C. A. (2005). An empirical study of individual competencies in distribution centers to enable continuous innovation. *Creativity & Innovation Management, 14*(3), 299-310.

Spears, L. C. (2004). Practicing servant-leadership. *Leader to Leader, 34*((Fall)), 7-11.

Spencer, L. M. & Spencer, S. M. (1993). *Competence at work : Models for superior performance*. New York, NY: Wiley.

Spencer, L. M., McClelland, D. C., & Spencer, S. M. (1994). *Competency assessment methods: History and state of the art*. Boston, MA: Hay/McBer Research Press.

Steinberg, R. J. (2006). Economic theories of nonprofit organizations. In W.W. Powell & R.J. Steinberg (Eds.), *The non-profit sector: A research handbook* (pp. 117-139). New Haven, CT: Yale University Press.

Steinberg, R. J. & Powell, W. W. (2006). Introduction. In W.W. Powell & R.J. Steinberg (Eds.), *The non-profit sector: A research handbook* (pp. 2-10). New Haven, CT: Yale University Press.

Sternberg, R. J. (1990). Prototypes of competence and incompetence. In R.J. Sternberg & Jr.J. Kolligian (Eds.), *Competence considered* (pp. 117-145). New Haven, CT: Yale University Press.

Sternberg, R. J. & Kolligian, Jr. J. (1990). In R.J. Sternberg & Jr.J. Kolligian (Eds.), *Competence considered* (pp. ix-xv). New Haven, CT: Yale University Press.

Sternberg, R. J. & Wagner, R. K. (1993). The g-ocentric view of intelligence and job performance is wrong. *Current Directions in Psychological Science, 2*(1), 1-5.

Strauss, R., Rosenheck, M., D'Aurelio, K., & Roseheim, J. (2008). Save the world, make a buck: Seven ideas from the nonprofit sector. *Chief Learning Officer, 7*(10), 30-35.

Teegarden, P. H. (2004). *Nonprofit executive leadership and transition survey 2004*. Retrieved from http://leadershiplearning.org/system/files/Nonprofit+Executive+Ldrshp+Transitions+Survey.pdf

Tierney, T. J. (2006). *The nonprofit sector's leadership deficit.* San Francisco.The Bridgespan Group

Tribe, D. (2001). Professional capability in the legal profession. In J. Raven & J. Stephenson (Eds.), *Competence in the learning society* (pp. 149-162). New York: Peter Lang.

Trochim, W. M. K. (2006). Positivism & post-positivism. Retrieved from http://www.socialresearchmethods. net/kb/positvsm.php

Tropman, J. E. & Shaefer, H. L. (2004). Flameout at the top-executive calamity in the nonprofit sector: Its precursors and sequelae. *Administration in Social Work, 28*(3/4), 161-182.

van der Klink, M. & Boon, J. (2002). The investigation of competencies within professional domains. *Human Resource Development International, 5*(4), 411.

Watson Wyatt Worldwide (2009a). *Effect of the economic crisis on employee attitudes towards retirement.* New York.Watson Wyatt Worldwide. Retrieved from http://www.watsonwyatt. com/research/deliverpdf.asp?catalog=WT-2009-12911

Watson Wyatt Worldwide (2009b). *Effect of the economic crisis on HR programs.* New York.Watson Wyatt Worldwide. Retrieved from http://www.watsonwyatt.com/research/ deliverpdf.asp?catalog=WT-2009-13754&id=x.pdf

Weitzman, M. S., Jalandoni, N. T., Lampkin, L. M., & Pollack, T. H. (2002). *The new nonprofit almanac & desk reference.* San Francisco, CA: Jossey-Bass.

Wells, D. W. (1988). Essential competencies for ACSI administrators: A national delphi study utilizing the toulmin unit of proof (Doctoral dissertation, University of Minnesota, 1988). *Dissertation Abstracts International, 49,* 07A, 1650.

Werther, Jr. W. B. (2004). Nonprofit organizations. In J.M. Burns, G.R. Geothal, & G.J. Sorenson (Eds.), *Encyclopedia of leadership*-(Vol. 3, pp. 1097-1102)). Thousand Oaks, CA: Sage.

White, R. W. (1959). Motivation reconsidered: The concept of competence. *Psychology Review, 66*(5), 297-333.

Williams, P. L. & Webb, C. (1994). The Delphi technique: A methodological discussion. *Journal of Advanced Nursing,* 19180-186.

Young, D. R. (2001b). Government failure theory. In S.J. Ott (Ed.), *The nature of the nonprofit sector* (pp. 190-193). Boulder, CO: Westview Press.

Young, D. R. (2001a). Contract failure theory. In S.J. Ott (Ed.), *The nature of the nonprofit sector* (pp. 193-196). Boulder, CO: Westview Press.

Yu-fen, C. & Tsui-chih, W. (2007). An empirical analysis of core competence for high-tech firms and traditional manufacturers. *Journal of Management Development, 26*(2), 159-168.

Zarinpoush, F. & Hall, M. H. (2007). *Leadership perspectives: Interviews with leaders of Canada's charities and nonprofit organizations.* Research Report Toronto, Canada.Imagine Canada. Retrieved from http://nonprofitscan.imaginecanada. ca/files/en/other_research/leadership_perspectives_08010 8.pdf

Zemke, R. & Zemke, S. (1999). Putting competencies to work. *Training, 36*(1), 70.

Zigarmi, D., Lyles, D., & Fowler, S. (2005). Context: The rosetta stone of leadership. *Leader to Leader, 38*(Fall 2005), 37-44.

Ziglio, E. (1996). The Delphi method and it contribution to decision-making. In M. Adler & E. Ziglio (Eds.), *Gazing into the oracle* (pp. 3-33). London, UK: Jessica Kingsley.

Appendix A

Preliminary Survey

Thank you for taking the time to complete this survey on your experience related to leadership in the nonprofit sector. This survey is part of a doctoral research project at Gonzaga University being conducted on leadership competency for nonprofit leaders.

As someone who have been involved in a variety of nonprofit organizations over the last 20 years and a student of leadership, I am concerned by the lack of attention given to nonprofit leadership. This doctoral project endeavors to develop a model that will aid in recruitment, training, and development of leaders for the nonprofit sector.

The information from this survey will be used to develop a better understanding of the unique challenges of leading in the nonprofit sector in the Northwest. There is also opportunity for those working in the nonprofit social service sector to participate in an additional focus group on this topic. You may indicate your interest at the end of this survey.

This survey should take only 10-15 minutes. Your participation is appreciated.

1. What is your current involvement with a nonprofit organization [501(c)(3) or 501(c)(4)]?

- [ ] Paid Staff
- [ ] Volunteer
- [ ] Board Member
- [ ] I have no current involvement

Other (please specify)

2. Is the organization with which you are currently involved a member organization of the Nonprofit Association of Oregon?

- ( ) Yes
- ( ) No

248

3. How much time per week do you work or volunteer in a nonprofit organization?

○ Less than 10 hours
○ 10 to 19 hours
○ 20 to 29 hours
○ 30 to 39 hours
○ 40 to 49 hours
○ More than 50 hours

Other (please specify)

5. Please give a very brief description of what you do.

6. How many years have you served with your CURRENT nonprofit organization as: (please round numbers to nearest whole i.e., 7.5 becomes 8)

Paid Staff

Volunteer

Board Member

7. How many years have you served in the nonprofit sector in general as: (please round your answer in the same manner as question 7)

Paid Staff

Volunteer

Board Member

8. Describe the population(s) or clientele your organization serves

9. Describe the services your organization provides

10. What are the goals or the mission of your current nonprofit organization? What are the organizations desired outcomes?

11. How many people are involved with your current nonprofit organization in each of the following catagories: (estimate if necessary)

Paid, full time employees (30+ hours per week)

Full time volunteers (30+ hours per week)

Paid, part time employees (less than 30 hours)

Part time volunteers (less than 30 hours)

12. Please rate the following regarding the significance of their contribution to the knowledge and skills required for your current position in the nonprofit sector.

	Very Significant	Significant	Somewhat Significant	Not Significant	N/A
Undergraduate education	○	○	○	○	○
Graduate education	○	○	○	○	○
Selected courses	○	○	○	○	○
Seminars or conferences	○	○	○	○	○
Interaction with colleagues	○	○	○	○	○
Informal mentoring	○	○	○	○	○
Formal mentoring	○	○	○	○	○
Previous roles in nonprofit organizations	○	○	○	○	○
On the job training	○	○	○	○	○

Other (please specify)

13. What is your educational background? Please list all degrees and certificates earned.

14. What type of additional training or education would be helpful to you in your current role?

15. What are the most significant challenges facing your organization?

16. Demographic Information - Gender

○ Male

○ Female

17. Demographic Information - Age

18. Would you be willing to participate in a study on leadership competencies for nonprofit leaders?

○ Yes

○ No

* 19. Please provide the following contact information. This information will only be retained in the event you that you participate in the competency study. Items with an asterisk (*) are required.

Name:*

Address:

Address 2:

City/Town:

State:

ZIP:

Email Address:*

Daytime Phone Number:

Thank you for taking the time to complete this survey. Your participation is greatly appreciated.

Appendix B

Research Stages Summary Table

Stages	Population	Survey Instrument	Type of data/response	Analysis of Responses
Preliminary Survey	Nonprofit Association of Oregon membership	Online Survey	Complete survey – *Quantitative*	Compile info – SPSS
Delphi Panel Round One	Selected Panel	Open-ended Question	Narrative or list format – *Qualitative*	Content/thematic analysis – NVivo
Delphi Panel Round Two	Respondents from previous round	Compiled results from previous round in list format – Rank/weight (quantitative) Rationale (qualitative)	Rank & Weight elements – *Quantitative*; Written rationale *Qualitative*	Statistical Analysis of rankings – SPSS Compile/edit rationales provided
Delphi Panel Round Three	Respondents from previous round	Compiled results from previous round in list format – Panelist reviews own ranking & is allowed to change previous responses	Rank & Weight elements – *Quantitative*; Written rationale for change in responses – *Qualitative*	Statistical Analysis of rankings – SPSS Analysis of response stability

Appendix C

Round One Instructions

Thank you for agreeing to participate in this of leadership competency for nonprofit leaders. Please review the following information about the purpose of the study and important terms. Next, respond to the Round One Question included at the end of this document. If you have any questions or concerns, please feel free to email me (compsurvey.vetter@gmail.com) or phone me at 503-589-8180 (work)/503-743-3761 (home).

Study Purpose
This research is designed to develop a competency model for executive leaders of social service agencies within the nonprofit sector. The models developed will be useful in the training, development, and recruitment of current and future leaders in this sector.

Procedures
Participants will be asked to respond to a series of questions over the course of three rounds of research. In each subsequent round students will be responding the results of the previous round with

the purpose of refining and moving towards a consensus on the leadership competencies for nonprofit leaders. Participants will be asked to carefully consider the information provided and to share their thoughts and perspectives. The desired outcome is to develop a model of competencies for those who lead social service agencies.

Definition of terms

Competencies

> These are specific statements that define areas of expertise viewed as essential for success in a given context. These would include competency characteristics or capabilities such as motives, traits, self-concept, knowledge, and skills (Spencer & Spencer, 1993, pp. 9-11). The motives and self-concept in competency include a self-awareness that includes a realistic view of personal strengths and weaknesses along with personal goals and values (Lowney, 2003, p. 98).

Competency models

> Competency models are the collection of competency statements for a given role that take into consideration not only behavioral aspects of leading, but also the necessary knowledge, skills, personal traits, and motives along with the organization's strategy and its implications for the leadership needs of the organization (Barner, 2000, p. 48; Boyatzis, 1983, p. 21, p. 35; Le Deist & Winterton, 2005, p. 33).

Social services agency within the nonprofit sector

A social services agency is a subsection of the nonprofit sector. The term "social services agency" is being used in reference to that portion of the nonprofit sector that provides services to the "deprived, neglected, or handicapped children and youth, the needy, elderly, the mentally ill and developmentally disabled, and disadvantaged adults. These services include daycare, counseling, job training, child protection, foster care, residential treatment, homemakers, rehabilitation, and sheltered workshops" (Smith, 2002, p. 153).

Delphi Panel Round One Question

Directions: Please answer the following question as completely as possible. Responses may take the form of short narrative or lists. Feel free to write as much as you choose or believe is necessary to clarify or explain your response. The purpose of this round is to explore the topic and identify competencies offered by the Delphi panel participants. Prior to answering the question, please read the study purpose and definition of terms. I would greatly appreciate if you could return your response by email or fax (503-585-8180) by March 14.

In your opinion, what are the skills, knowledge, traits, motives, and self-concept/self-understanding that are essential for executive-level leaders in nonprofit, social services organizations?

- Skills—What must the leader be able to do?

- Knowledge—What must the leader know?

- Traits—What personal characteristics contribute to role success?

- Motives—What motivates the leader? What causes an individual to fully engage in their work?

- Self-concept/self-understandings—How does the leader view themselves, their role, and others?

- Other

Appendix D

Define Competencies from Round One

Compiled Round One Results

Skills—What must the leader be able to do?

Communication/Listening

- Communicate well with board, managers, the public and line staff
- Over-communicate Organizational Clarity (helping employees and core stakeholders understand where the organization is going and what purpose it serves)
- How to articulate the mission
- Clearly and concisely restate problems and concerns
- Strong communicator/Direct communication skills
- Effective communication skills—be a really good listener, ability to articulate a vision that others can follow, strong in oral and written communication

- It's my job to listen to people carefully. Even listening for what's not being said.
- It is essential that a non-profit leader possess excellent communication, presentation, and management skills.
- An ED (Executive Director) must be able to communicate effectively and with compassion whether speaking to a staff member, a four-year old child who has suffered abuse, an agency representative desperately seeking support, or a top level executive who may be a prospective board member.
- The ability to be outgoing, to listen effectively
- Written and verbal communication

Problem solving
- Problem solving techniques

Building/Managing a Team
- Build the management team/Team building techniques
- To facilitate the team and its discussions.
- Personnel management—know how to give clear direction and communicate expectations; hold people accountable for their responsibilities; praise when they are doing their job well
- Some, but necessarily all of the jobs of the people he/she supervises
- Leaders must know how to hire great people/How to recruit the right people for key positions
- How all jobs are to be performed and what every ones weaknesses and strengths are.
- Know how to motivate staff and volunteers.

- Remove the barriers and obstacles that are keeping my team from moving forward on their goals.
- Empower team members to take on increasing levels of responsibility and decision making authority.
- A healthy organization is the sum of its parts; the leader's role is to make all those parts work in harmony. A leader's role is to help everyone in the organization identify their own strengths and leverage those strengths into action.
- The leader's role includes bringing a sense of confidence to others.
- It is essential that a nonprofit leader possess excellent communication, presentation, and management skills.
- Within the organization itself, a good leader must rally the talents of employees and direct them successfully toward the mission or goal set forth.
- Ability to gather many different personality types and find a common ground that will unite them and inspire them is essential.

Empathy/Compassion
- Genuinely care about the organization, people and issues

Organizational Planning & Development
- Create Organizational clarity (mission, vision, purpose, values)
- Create systems that reinforce the organizational clarity (hiring, firing, pay raises, reviews, training, etc.)

- Planning know how to assess program effectiveness and show measurable outcomes of success. Develop feedback models to determine areas of strengths and weakness.
- Create a planning organization, one that works efficiently with the resources available to achieve the mission
- Ability to understand the relationship to the organizations mission
- Understand organizational structure, policies and culture
- Understand organization and the people he/she leads
- Leaders must know how to create and communicate organizational clarity
- The goals and functions of the nonprofit/How to keep the organization on mission
- Strategic planning processes/ability to plan carefully
- Adequate and appropriate policies and procedures
- How to change and adapt
- The mission must be carefully determined following research and study with regard to the needs of the community we serve.

Financial Management & Development

- Financial Management—must understand how to read financial statements, develop budgets, understand cash flow projections, prepare financial reports for various audiences (board, funders)
- Budgeting and financial basics
- Grant-seeking basics and knowledge of sources for grants or other programs that help nonprofits

- Stewardship—know how the agency is funded, what the future projections for the funding are, know how to develop a diverse funding base, different strategies to increase revenue.
- Adequate funding

Respect for people

- Genuinely care about the organization, people and issues
- Ability to relate to people
- Respects the value of others
- Respect of diverse people and their opinions

Relationships outside the organization

- Respect of the community
- Build partnerships
- The community and its needs
- Community-minded
- He/she must also address the community at large and engage them on all levels—as donors, volunteers, corporate leaders, teachers, law enforcement, government, recipients, and strangers to our cause.
- To effectively carry out the duties of a nonprofit ED, one must know the community, people, geography, work force, corporate leaders, business, non-profit organizations—working knowledge of everything that makes a community function.
- Know our politicians and what they stand for; understand teachers and the health of our schools; interact with businesses and learn how to partner with them, know the elder population and how to interact with them—every faction of our society has

functions, needs and something to offer. An ED's job is to know how to bring all these factions together to compel and inspire, discussion, partnership, action, and positive outcomes.

- The industry/field(s) represented by the organization
- Must know their stakeholders

Decision Maker

- Leadership—ability to be decisive when needed and flexible when needed and ability to recognize which is called for in the moment
- They often stand alone when the hard work and/or decision need to be made, but stand with all when success occurs.

Leadership Perspective

- Think of the nonprofit and its mission, rather than their own agendas
- See the big picture
- Be positive and support the majority vote process.
- Manage time and juggle many responsibilities
- What must the leader know?

Board Function & Development

- Know how boards work, how to create a strong partnership with the agency's board of directors.
- Governance-understand the policies, laws, rules that relate to the organization's mission to ensure compliance.
- Supportive board
- Trusting board and staff

- A good ED is able to form and lead a board of directors effectively—bringing together a diverse group of talented community member who will enter into service energetically and leave that service a better person.
- A leader must possess knowledge of board members to engage them fully

Information/Learning Skills

- A variety of computer programs
- Learn quickly
- Leaders have to know where to get the information they need to make decisions.
- Research capabilities
- Learning theory
- Inter-disciplinary
- Willingness to always learn more/How to keep learning
- Thirst for lifelong learning
- Education is continuous

Legal & Operational Requirements

- Legal and fiduciary responsibilities
- Industry standards, current trends and potential future direction
- Labor and personnel laws
- Insurance requirements
- Business: HR, finance, legal, facilities, development

Conflict Resolution & Mediation

- How to be impartial
- Mediation procedures

Spokesperson & Cheerleader

- Ambassadorship—know how to tell the story of the organization in a way that invites people to be engaged.
- Celebrate the successes,
- Talk about the compelling need and the unique response to resolve it
- Be able to speak for the group and give credit, where it's due.
- They are the team cheer leader.
- Lighten staff fears

Traits—What personal characteristics contribute to role success?

Team Orientation

- Work as a team member
- Open-minded
- Inclusive
- Consensus seeking
- Collaborative
- Whatever the success or the achievements, they know and recognize the teamwork involved.
- Think and say "We" and not "I"
- They often stand alone when the hard work and/or decision need to be made, but stand with all when success occurs. An ED will feel fortunate to be a part of a team that is well

functioning and thus integral to the success of the community as a whole.

Patience/Perseverance

- Patience—take the long term perspective, know that this too shall pass, stay focused on the vision
- Perseverance—exercise willpower to stay with it especially when it looks impossible

Personal Traits

- Spirited
- Giving
- Enthusiastic/joyful/positive
- A good leader is confident, yet self-less.
- Passion and energy
- Good-natured
- Observant
- Genuine
- Fully engaged in life
- Dedication/loyalty
- Optimism-social service agencies often work with people in difficult situations. It is important for the leader to role model a healthy perspective on life.
- Honesty/integrity is essential.
- Common sense
- Being reasonable

Work/Professional Traits

- Flexible/adaptive
- Dependable/reliability
- Empowering
- Level headed
- Good leader ship skills
- Good at delegating
- Consistency
- Accountability
- Knowledgeable/competent/intelligent
- Creative/idea person
- Role model desired behaviors
- Fairness
- Resourceful
- A good leader must be pragmatic, diplomatic
- A balance of goal and relationship focus

Interpersonal Skills/Traits

- Social intelligence—ability to consider another's perspective, understand where they are coming from, adapt message and/or communication style to effectively work with others
- Personable
- Caring/generous
- Welcoming/open/friendly
- Heartfelt
- People person
- Appreciative
- Agreeable

- Supportive/cooperative/helpful
- Patient and yet forthright

Motives –What motivates the leader? What causes an individual to fully engage in their work?

Commitment to the Mission/Purpose

- Passion for the mission of the organization
- The goals of the nonprofit
- When you believe, really believe in your organization's mission, motivation follows. And in order to believe, you must take the time to get in the trenches and see and feel with your own senses
- Shared vision for the organization
- Passion

Fair Compensation

- *No responses*

Meaningful Work/Seeing Results

- A sense of right livelihood, a firm belief in the agency's mission, a desire to improve circumstances for others.
- I am motivated by knowing my work has meaning and purpose.
- Feeling like you are making a difference
- I know that the work I do matters to others and because of that, I give it everything.
- The desire to make a difference—the longevity of past results

- Recognizing what one's strengths are and having the joy of putting them to use is very motivating.
- Past work experiences especially successes
- Seeing the impact of their efforts
- Inclusion in the planning and decision making
- Love the work
- When you engage the public, lead the action, and begin to see positive outcomes, the motivation continues.
- Accomplishment, sense of fulfillment
- Understands their life's work in terms of calling, and that a calling is not just a particular job

Personal Values

- Spiritual beliefs/personal spiritual faith
- I believe this (motivation) has to come from within.

Relationship with Colleagues

- Outstanding staff/co-workers
- I work harder knowing that others are counting on me. I work to live up to the expectations of my board and my friends, and my employees.
- Everyone's excitement and motivation to make a difference.
- Thanks/praise

Enjoyment of Administrative Work

- A nonprofit leader is responsible for such a variety of tasks, the right person must enjoy the breadth of the work, as it is difficult to deeply immerse in specific areas.
- Enjoyment of administrative work

Self-concept/self-understandings—How does the leader view him- or herself, his/her role, and others?

Humble
- I believe an effective leader views themselves with humility.
- I am the servant. The more people I hire, the more people I report to.
- No ego
- Essentially, a leader knows that humility is a key attribute, as is the ability to know that teamwork leads to success and every thriving team has a great leader.
- A balance of self-confidence and humility

Takes Responsibility for the development & success of the organization
- I am the final decision maker, although I do gather ideas and opinions from staff, board, and customers before making a decision.
- My primary responsibility is to the organization and its long-term health. My secondary responsibility is to the staff. My tertiary responsibility is to our customers.

- The leader is responsible for clarifying the vision, mission, and goals (developed by all members of the organization), keeping these alive and in the forefront, reminding others of the purpose of the work.
- I am the visionary. I look to the future and I ask why we do things in our current manner. Is there a better way that we are missing?
- I am a teacher...the more quickly I can make my job obsolete, the sooner I can move on to other higher level work.
- Assume responsibility for decisions and communication

Outcomes Focus/Results Oriented

- The leader has the hardest role. They must represent the entire team with their own work ethics.
- Hard-working, perhaps even driven
- Goal focused
- Consistent work ethic
- Produce results
- Determined
- Opportunistic
- The ability to execute plans successfully
- Nonprofit leaders oftentimes must be able to enter a situation of complete hopelessness and from the ashes create renewal and hope and positive outcomes where none had been seen or imagined.

Self assured/Confident/Self-aware

- Grounded
- Composed
- Be willing to listen to criticism and corrections as well, as offer praise to others.
- Self-confidence - composure under stress
- Independent
- Assertiveness
- Knows what they don't know and how to staff their weakness
- Understands that they are not just the role, the job is not who they are
- Understands that supportive relationships are essential but that ultimately, the only one responsible for their spiritual, emotional and physical health is themselves

Other

- I don't think it matters if you are a leader of a social service organization, a small business, a corporation, or an arts non-profit. I think good business leadership skills transcend industry boundaries.
- Much depends on the size of the organization. In smaller agencies, the leader is responsible for doing much of the service work in addition to the larger overview piece. In larger agencies, the leader needs different skills such as political savvy.

- For a Christian leader in a ministry role it is essential to continually seek to discern the difference between meeting others' expectations and pleasing God.

Comments from Traits sections:

- I think this varies greatly by the person. Any personal characteristic carries with it a benefit and a drawback. I personally think humility is important, but many great leaders lack humility. Others might see strong organizational skills as a plus, but some people are great leaders without being at all organized. Steve Jobs is a highly creative, highly driven leader. But he can be arrogant and difficult to work with. He's still very effective.

Appendix E

Round Two Instructions

Delphi Panel Round Two—Summary & Instructions

Thank you for thoughtful input to the first round question regarding leadership competency. The question you were asked to respond to was:

In your opinion, what are the skills, knowledge, traits, motives, and self-concept/self-understanding that are essential for executive-level leaders in nonprofit, social services organizations?

The input from all participants was compiled and prepared for further input from everyone. You will find the following documents enclosed for the second round of the study.

- A set of instructions and directions (this document)
- An overview of the study and its purpose as reminder (this document).

- An eight (8) page document, Compiled Round One Results, under each of the main headings used in the first round: skills, knowledge, traits, etc.
- A spreadsheet listing all the competencies identified in Round One to be used for ranking and weighting (Ranking Document).
- A sample of a spreadsheet showing how to complete the ranking & weighting (Sample Ranking Document).
- Each panelist is also receiving a copy of their own responses to the question from the first round to use for review or comparison as needed.

Round Two Summary

In this round you have opportunity respond to the results from Round One. You are free to add more competencies if you feel something is missing or comment on what others have submitted. You can also add comments to clarify your own input from Round One. Again, you can also feel free to add competencies you feel may be missing.

The process of compiling the results from Round One required that the researcher make some decisions on the competency category names, how many categories, and what should be included in each category. This process, while informed by other studies and literature on competency models, sought to bring forward and use the language introduced by you, the panelists as much as possible.

In many cases the competency category names selected are the actual words used by someone on the panel; in other cases category names were created to summarize or encapsulate the essence of what was submitted by the panel. As you read the competency categories and the material in each, please note:

- The order in which the competencies categories appear under each heading does not suggest any type of ranking of importance.
- The text used as the descriptions/definitions for each competency category is the responses from the panel. Duplicate material has been removed for the sake of brevity.
- The competency categories under the skills and knowledge in some ways could be viewed as interchangeable. The general expectation is that a person does what they know, and what they know, they are expected to act on (skill).
- There were cases where items were mentioned by one panelist under one category (skill, trait, etc.) and the same item was placed in another category by another panelist. The researcher placed such items into a single category based on the **majority** placement of the panel members. Items may have been rearranged in this way but no items have been eliminated.

Round Two Instructions

In this round you are being asked to do four things:

1. Review the Compiled Round One Results document. Add any comments you see as necessary and other competencies as well.

2. Use the spreadsheet provided to rank each competency under the categories of Skills, Knowledge, Traits, Motives, and Self Concept. This is a numerical ranking, beginning with 1 as the most important, and then rank each item in the category.

3. In addition to ranking items, you are asked to assign a weight to each item in the category. The single item that you believe should receive the lowest importance will be assigned a 10 on a scale of 10 -100. Each additional item will be assigned a weighting between 10 and 100 based on how important you feel that item may be. You should not use a number more than once. This weighting will be used to further investigate the importance of each item relative to its ranking by all panelists. Each category (skills, knowledge, etc.) should be weighted separately.

4. The last step is to rank, in the far right column of the spreadsheet, what you believe to be the top 15 items (1-15 with 1 being most important). You may choose from any of the 30 competencies listed under each category.

Please review the sample spreadsheet before beginning your ranking and weighting. If you have questions please do not hesitate to contact me. I would be more than happy to give further explanation. Prior to answering the question, please read the study purpose and definition of terms. I would greatly appreciate if you could return your response by **April 25, 2011**. If you have any questions or concerns, please feel free to email me (compsurvey.vetter@gmail.com) or phone me at 503-589-8180 (work)/503-743-3761 (home).

Appendix F

Round Three Instructions

Delphi Panel Round Three—Summary & Instructions

Thank you for participation through the first two rounds. As a reminder, the original question you were asked to respond to was:

In your opinion, what are the skills, knowledge, traits, motives, and self-concept/self-understanding that are essential for executive-level leaders in nonprofit, social services organizations?

The results of the first round were compiled placed in to five categories (skills, knowledge, traits, motives, and self-concept/self- understanding) for review by the panel. In the second round you were asked to do three things:

1. Rank each item in the five categories beginning with the number one (1) signifying the competency you viewed as most important in that category and assigning a number until all items were ranked.
2. Assign each item in the category a weighting from 10-100.

3. Drawing from the complete list of 30 competencies, you were asked to choose what you viewed to be the top15 and assign a numerical ranking (1-15) with one being the most important.

The input from all participants was compiled and prepared for further review and input from the rest of the expert panel. You will find the following documents enclosed for the third and final round of the study.

- A set of instructions and directions (this document)
- An overview of the study and its purpose as reminder (this document).
- An eight (8) page document, Compiled Round One Results, by categories under each of the main headings used in the first round: skills, knowledge, traits, etc. This is to refresh your memory on the items from the first round that aided in the creation of the various categories.
- Two spreadsheets for you to review and add revisions or comments as you see feel are needed. The two spreadsheets are:
  - Ranking & Weightings by Category—this is the compilation of rankings and weightings within each category. The categories are sorted with the competency ranked highest by the panel first.
  - Top 15 Competencies—all the competencies are shown in order of ranking based on the rankings provided by the panel.

Round Three Summary

In this third and final round you have opportunity respond to the results from Round Two. You are being asked to review the group results and your own responses in light of the group averages. In each of the spreadsheets you will see the group average, your own responses from Round Two (no other panel members have access to your individual scores) and a column for you to revise your responses. You are also free to add comments or thoughts related to what you are seeing in the results from Round Two.

The following working definitions are provided to provide a common understanding of terms used on the spreadsheets.

- **Average Rank/Weighting**—this is the mathematical average or mean of all the rankings or weightings provided.
  - The **lower** the average **ranking** the **more important** the item.
  - The **higher** the average **weighting**, the **more importance** was placed on that particular item.
- The significance of the weighting score is that it serves as a secondary measure of importance by helping the researcher to evaluate more closely the relationship between ranked items. For example, the fictitious results below show Red Umbrellas as having the highest **Ranking Average** (1st column) at 1.23 which made it first in the category followed by Green Umbrellas (2.33) and finally Blue Umbrellas (2.89). This is self-explanatory. The **Weighting Average** helps the reader to see that the interval or the distance between items may not be as

uniform as one may be lead to believe by simply looking at a 1-3 ranked order. What the weighting average reveals is that the difference in the interval or distance between Red Umbrellas (ranked 1st) and Green umbrellas (2nd) is less than the interval or Green Umbrellas and Blue Umbrellas (3rd). What this reveals is a greater interval between umbrella types 2 & 3 (63.54 & 31.11) than there is between types 1 & 2 (74.6 & 63.54). The weighting averages actually show that items one and two in the list (Red & Green Umbrellas) are very close in importance. Blue Umbrellas are a distant third. This is how the weighting can add another layer to the understanding of importance to the rankings.

	Ranking Aver	StdDev	Category Ranking	Weighting Aver	StdDev
Red Umbrellas	1.23	.78	1	74.60	32.02
Green Umbrellas	2.33	1.24	2	63.54	35.54
Blue Umbrellas	2.89	1.63	3	31.11	38.55

- **Standard Deviation** (StdDev)—this is a measure of the variance of the all the response. The higher the standard deviation the greater the difference in the response provided by the panel. In the example above Blue Umbrellas have a standard deviation of 1.63. This means there was a not a lot of agreement on this item. Some people have scored it high and others scored it low. This shows a lack on consensus among the panel. When looking at standard deviation it is important to remember the scale or range of values being considered. Again, in the example above the category rankings span from 1-3 while the weighting can range from 10-100 which means a larger standard deviation should be expected.

- I would be happy to speak with you via phone or answer questions about the stats via email to clear up any questions you may have. Please don't hesitate to ask.

Round Three Instructions

In this round you are being asked to do four things:

1. Review the Compiled Round Two Results documents (two spreadsheets).

2. The spreadsheet for Ranking & Weighting has columns showing the group averages, the standard deviation, your Ranking/Weighting, and finally a column where you can make revisions to your score based on the group score. You can change as many or as few of your ranking or weightings as you choose to. Please make changes in the column marked Revised Rankings or Revised Weighting.

3. On the sheet labeled Top 15 please do two things:

   a. Review your own rankings in light of the group response. Adjust as you see fit. Again, if you would like to add comments that would be acceptable.

   b. Weight your **REVISED** the top 15 competencies. Rank the item you feel has the least importance as a 10 and then weight the remaining 14 competencies with numbers up to 100 but without reusing any single number. Be sure to weight the lowest item as 10. If you have questions please do not hesitate to contact me. I would be more than happy to give further explanation.

4. Feel free to include comments or thoughts on why you have ranked and weighted items in comparison with the rest of the group.

I would greatly appreciate if you could return your response by **June 20, 2011**. If you have any questions or concerns, please feel free to email me (compsurvey.vetter@gmail.com) or phone me at 503-589-8180 (work)/503-743-3761 (home).

Study Purpose

This research is designed to develop a competency model for executive leaders of social service agencies within the nonprofit sector. The models developed will be useful in the training, development, and recruitment of current and future leaders in this sector.

Procedures

Participants will be asked to respond to a series of questions over the course of three rounds of research. In each subsequent round students will be responding the results of the previous round with the purpose of refining and moving towards a consensus on the leadership competencies for nonprofit leaders.

Participants will be asked to carefully consider the information provided and to share their thoughts and perspectives. The desired outcome is to develop a model of competencies for those who lead social service agencies.

Definition of terms

Competencies

These are specific statements that define areas of expertise viewed as essential for success in a given context. These would include competency characteristics or capabilities such as motives, traits, self-concept, knowledge, and skills (Spencer & Spencer, 1993, pp. 9-11). The motives and self-concept in competency include a self-awareness that includes a realistic view of personal strengths and weaknesses along with personal goals and values (Lowney, 2003, p. 98).

Competency models

Competency models are the collection of competency statements for a given role that take into consideration not only behavioral aspects of leading, but also the necessary knowledge, skills, personal traits, and motives along with the organization's strategy and its implications for the leadership needs of the organization (Barner, 2000, p. 48; Boyatzis, 1983, p. 21, p. 35; Le Deist & Winterton, 2005, p. 33).

Social services agency within the nonprofit sector

A social services agency is a subsection of the nonprofit sector. The term "social services agency" is being used in reference to that portion of the nonprofit sector that provides services to the "deprived, neglected, or handicapped children and youth, the needy, elderly, the mentally ill and developmentally disabled, and disadvantaged adults. These services include daycare, counseling, job training, child protection, foster care, residential treatment, homemakers, rehabilitation, and sheltered workshops" (Smith, 2002, p. 153).

20230161R00162

Made in the USA
San Bernardino, CA
03 April 2015